ASHE Higher Education Report: Volume 38, Number 3
Kelly Ward, Lisa E. Wolf-Wendel, Series Editors

Assessing Meaning Making and Self-Authorship: Theory, Research, and Application

Marcia B. Baxter Magolda

Patricia M. King

Discover this journal online at
wileyonlinelibrary.com

Assessing Meaning Making and Self-Authorship: Theory, Research, and Application
Marcia B. Baxter Magolda and Patricia M. King
ASHE Higher Education Report: Volume 38, Number 3
Kelly Ward, Lisa E. Wolf-Wendel, Series Editors

Cover image by a_Taiga/©iStockphoto.

ISSN 1551-6970   electronic ISSN 1554-6306   ISBN 978-1-1185-0054-5

The ASHE Higher Education Report is part of the Jossey-Bass Higher and Adult Education Series and is published six times a year by Wiley Subscription Services, Inc., A Wiley Company, at Jossey-Bass, One Montgomery Street, Suite 1200, San Francisco, California 94104-4594.

For subscription information, see the Back Issue/Subscription Order Form in the back of this volume.

CALL FOR PROPOSALS: Prospective authors are strongly encouraged to contact Kelly Ward (kaward@wsu.edu) or Lisa Wolf-Wendel (lwolf@ku.edu). See "About the ASHE Higher Education Report Series" in the back of this volume.

Visit the Jossey-Bass Web site at **www.josseybass.com.**

Printed in the United States of America on acid-free recycled paper.

The ASHE Higher Education Report is indexed in CIJE: Current Index to Journals in Education (ERIC), Education Index/Abstracts (H.W. Wilson), ERIC Database (Education Resources Information Center), Higher Education Abstracts (Claremont Graduate University), IBR & IBZ: International Bibliographies of Periodical Literature (K.G. Saur), and Resources in Education (ERIC).

Advisory Board

The ASHE Higher Education Report Series is sponsored by the Association for the Study of Higher Education (ASHE), which provides an editorial advisory board of ASHE members.

Contents

Executive Summary

Learning to think critically and in a complex way about a wide range of issues, demonstrating intercultural competence when interacting with others, and making discerning judgments about moral and ethical issues are common learning goals in higher education. Learners often struggle to achieve these goals because they have yet to develop the meaning-making capacities that support their achievement. Meaning-making capacities reflect how people make sense of (or interpret) their experience, including their assumptions about how to decide what to believe, construct their identities, and engage in relationships with others. The complex meaning-making capacity of self-authorship, characterized by the ability to internally coordinate external influence in the process of defining one's beliefs, identity, and social relations, forms a basis for meeting the complex challenges that college students and other adults face as they navigate life. To assist learners in developing these meaning-making capacities, educators need to understand how these capacities evolve and how to assess learners' meaning making.

This monograph is designed to help its readers understand how the capacity for complex meaning making evolves from late adolescence to early adulthood and how this capacity is reflected in (and undergirds) how students make sense of their experiences. Readers who understand the role of meaning making will be better able to document its effects on educational outcomes and provide better information to decision makers about program effectiveness. Our collective scholarship on student development and assessment supports self-authorship as a necessary but insufficient condition for achieving complex college learning outcomes. Thus, increased ability to assess self-authorship development can contribute to educators' efforts to understand, document, and promote these learning outcomes.

Our long-standing research programs addressing the assessment of cognitive development—Baxter Magolda's (1992) Epistemological Reflection Model and King and Kitchener's (1994) Reflective Judgment Model—undergird our work on assessing self-authorship. As co-principal investigators of the Wabash National Study of Liberal Arts Education (WNS), we designed a four-year longitudinal study of contemporary college students' meaning making informed by Baxter Magolda's twenty-five-year longitudinal study of young adult development. Over one thousand interviews from Baxter Magolda's study and over nine hundred WNS interviews enable us to describe a detailed portrait of the evolution of meaning making during and after college from a diverse group of participants. In this monograph, we show how young adults' capacities become more complex and adaptive over time and describe the strategies we have developed to assess and document these changes.

The nuanced portrait of self-authorship development that emerged from these two studies offers numerous possibilities regarding the complexity of development from the late teens to the early forties across three dimensions: cognitive (How do I know?), intrapersonal (Who am I?), and interpersonal (How do I relate to others?). From this rich data set, we discerned a continuum of ten positions within three overarching meaning-making structures. The first three positions (comprising the first major meaning-making structure: External meaning making) portray variations of trusting external authorities to define one's beliefs, identity, and social relations. The middle four positions (the Crossroads: the second major structure) illustrate movement away from uncritical reliance on external authority and simultaneous movement toward constructing one's internal voice to coordinate external influence. The last three positions portray self-authorship, or trusting one's internal voice to guide one's life (the third structure: Internal meaning making). The ten positions and the rich narratives through which we describe them offer both researchers and educators greater insight into how adults approach learning, their identities, and their social relations.

A key facet of assessing self-authorship is that it requires discerning the distinctions between how people think (meaning-making structure) and what they think (content). In addition, meaning-making structures evolve gradually and often overlap; people may use more than one structure simultaneously or various structures depending on the context; and meaning-making structures may vary across the cognitive, intrapersonal, and interpersonal dimensions of development. We have constructed self-authorship interviews and an accompanying Self-Authorship Assessment Guide to address these complexities. We include the Guide in this monograph to assist readers in understanding the nuances of assessing the evolution of self-authorship. We also describe the process we used to train the WNS qualitative research team of over sixty graduate students and professionals to assess meaning making.

We hope this nuanced portrait of the developmental journey toward self-authorship, the detailed Assessment Guide, and our story of using this Guide with a large research team will provide educators and researchers with processes to understand, assess, and promote young adults' meaning-making capacities.

Foreword

There has been a lot of talk about the need to assess student learning outcomes. Colleges and universities across the country are scrambling to find the means to show that they are making a difference in student learning. Their concern is prompted by accreditation efforts, efforts by national associations (for example, the Voluntary System of Accountability authored by the Association of Public and Land-Grant Universities and the Association of State Colleges and Universities), and published critiques of higher education (books like *Academically Adrift: Limited Learning on College Campuses, Higher Education?,* and others). The question on everyone's mind is, How do we know if college is making a difference in student learning? This monograph provides a tool to help answer part of this question through the lens of meaning making and self-authorship. Self-authorship, one of my favorite student development concepts, is centered on how individuals make sense of information around them and use that information to help inform how they make decisions and, in turn, figure out who they are as a result. Unlike other student development theories, self-authorship and the process of meaning making represent a holistic approach to development. As a theory it does more than look at cognition or moral judgments or identity separately; rather, it combines these aspects into a single lens. I find the theory useful because it shows how people evolve from late adolescence to adulthood and is therefore relevant to a wide array of today's students, including graduate students.

When Marcia Baxter Magolda and Patricia King contacted me about their writing a monograph on self-authorship and meaning making as a means to explain how it can be assessed and used more easily by colleges and universities as an outcome, I was elated. A monograph that not only explains the theory in depth but also talks about how it can be assessed and documented as a learning outcome was more than I could have hoped for. This monograph delivers on its initial promise. The authors bring their expertise as the authors of the Epistemological Reflection Model (Baxter Magolda, 1992) and the Reflective Judgment Model (King and Kitchener, 1994), along with interviews from almost two thousand students, to explain how meaning making and self-authorship develop throughout the college experience and into adulthood. The authors lay out a new conceptualization of developmental meaning making that extends beyond what they have written before. They offer a more finely grained portrait of development (what they call positions) to enable readers to understand meaning making and its role in student learning. The inclusion of the training component and the Assessment Guide are new, detailed resources; both are aimed at making this process accessible for readers to use in their own work. Thus, the application component focuses on assessment practice, that is, how to gather information to inform the design of educational practice.

Although meaning making is not a typical learning outcome, the ability to identify the lack of complex meaning making may be a potential reason for students' underperforming on other outcome measures. Meaning making in general, and self-authorship in particular, is seen as necessary but insufficient for numerous collegiate outcomes, including critical thinking. This monograph explains how meaning-making capacities (including the capacity of self-authorship) relate to and are distinct from collegiate outcomes and explains how an understanding of meaning-making structures can contribute to facilitating student learning.

This book is written for scholars of higher education as well as for faculty and administrators. It will be of particular interest to assessment specialists who are interested in understanding self-authorship and its assessment and using it in their own work. It will also be of use to those of us who teach graduate classes in higher education administration or student affairs. The monograph expertly combines extensive discussions of theory and its creation, along with a helpful guide to assessing self-authorship and meaning making. While meaning making may not be the only outcome that needs to be assessed, it is an important one because it has the capacity to capture what happens in class along with what happens outside the classroom. This is a thoughtful, exciting addition to the ASHE Higher Education Report Series. I hope it is as enlightening to you as it was to me.

Lisa E. Wolf-Wendel
Series Editor

Acknowledgments

A project of this scope requires many sources of insight and substantial resources. We are deeply appreciative of the support, involvement, and constructive feedback provided by our communities of scholars. Because of the centrality of the Self-Authorship Assessment Guide in this monograph, we begin by noting that the refinement of this Guide has been a team effort, one informed by the insights of many individuals. In particular, we wish to acknowledge the contributions of several colleagues who made particularly strong and sustained contributions to refining this Guide. Three are former or current doctoral students from the University of Michigan: James P. Barber (now at the College of William and Mary), Anat Levtov (now at Bowling Green State University), and Rosemary J. Perez. Kari B. Taylor (associate director for student development for the University Honors Program at Miami University) also contributed many thoughtful insights about ways to capture developmental nuances within this Guide. She also played a major role in conveying development in visual form through the conceptualization of Figure 1; for this we appreciate her resourcefulness and patience. We thank Kelsey Chun, a Miami University student, whose artistic talent translated this conceptualization into Figure 1.

Many of the ideas presented here have been introduced at professional conferences and enriched by the questions and comments of colleagues and discussants. Most relevant to this monograph are two papers presented at annual meetings of the Association for the Study of Higher Education. The first (Baxter Magolda, King, Taylor, and Perez, 2008) was our initial attempt to identify more finely grained steps in initial meaning-making structures; these ideas are incorporated in the chapter "Trusting External Authority: External Positions." The second (King, Baxter Magolda, Perez, and Taylor, 2009) also focused on identifying more finely grained developmental steps in intermediate meaning-making structures; these ideas are incorporated in chapters "Entering the Crossroads: Predominantly External Positions" and "Leaving the Crossroads: Predominantly Internal Positions." In each paper, Rosemary Perez and Kari Taylor made substantive contributions and were fully involved in constructing the manuscripts, as they also did in the chapters of this monograph they coauthored. Here, we express our appreciation for the care and rigor with which they challenged ideas and crafted responses that ultimately strengthened these chapters.

We also express our appreciation to James P. Barber for his sustained interest in the training of interviewers and summarizers for the Wabash National Study of Liberal Arts Education (WNS). He not only coordinated the logistical elements of this annual process but also generously shared his own mistakes for training purposes and offered many well-grounded insights about the process of learning to assess development. Many of these appear in the chapter "Development of the Ten Positions in the Journey Toward Self-Authorship," which he coauthored.

The qualitative portion of the WNS would not have been possible without our research team of graduate and undergraduate students, as well as professional staff from the University of Michigan, Miami University, the University of Iowa, the Center of Inquiry in the Liberal Arts at Wabash College, Eastern Michigan University, Virginia Tech University, and Indiana University. These sixty-eight people (listed in the appendix) participated in annual training, offered their insights to refine the interview and data analysis processes, conducted and summarized over nine hundred interviews, assisted with data management, and provided many types of administrative support. We are grateful for their commitment and contributions to this project.

As we emphasize throughout this monograph, developmental assessment requires specialized knowledge and skills. The complexities associated with identifying and describing this process also required significant financial resources. We are particularly grateful to Charlie Blaich and his colleagues at the Center of Inquiry in the Liberal Arts at Wabash College for their support of the qualitative portion of the WNS. This support not only enabled the launch of one of the largest longitudinal qualitative projects of college student learning and development conducted to date, but it enabled researchers to conduct mixed-methods research on important questions of college impact and the identification of educational practices that promote learning and development. Our collaboration with Ernest Pascarella, principal investigator for the quantitative portion of the WNS, and the University of Iowa research team enriched our work. We are particularly grateful to Kathy Goodman and Tricia Seifert for their contributions to our mixed-methods work, which helped triangulate the qualitative findings.

Several other offices offered financial support that enabled data collection for this project. We gratefully acknowledge the support of the following offices at the University of Michigan: the Office of the Vice President for Research, the Horace Rackham Graduate School, the School of Education, and the Center for the Study of Higher and Postsecondary Education. The National Center for Institutional Diversity also provided support for a study examining the link between self-authorship and the development of a key learning outcome, intercultural maturity (Perez, Shim, King, and Baxter Magolda, 2011). We gratefully acknowledge the support of Miami University's School of Education, Health, and Society. In addition, the support of the administrators and staff members from the six interview campuses was essential to launching our data collection efforts; we thank them for their coordination of on-campus interviews and accommodating the visiting interview teams.

We close with a final note of thanks to those who really made this monograph possible: the participants of Baxter Magolda's ongoing study of adult development and the students in the interview sample of the WNS. Thank you for so candidly sharing the ups and downs of your collegiate and post-collegiate experiences with us! We have learned so much from you and promise to honor our commitment to using these insights to improve educational experiences for others.

Published online in Wiley Online Library
(wileyonlinelibrary.com) • DOI: 10.1002/aehe.20003

Nudging Minds to Life: Self-Authorship as a Foundation for Learning

F IGURING OUT HOW TO BE A GOOD STUDENT in college is a
complicated process: the instructions are often ambiguous, the content
is challenging, course readings use unfamiliar styles and genres, professors have
different expectations about skills they expect students to demonstrate, and
just when students master one skill, they learn that these skills do not apply
in the same way with another instructor or are not relevant in another disci-
pline. Furthermore, the culture of the campus may be quite foreign, and a student's taken-for-granted ways of talking with peers, interacting with
instructors, and even choosing how to dress may suddenly be called into question. Somehow students are expected to figure out how to respond to shifting
contexts and expectations. Similarly, figuring out how to be a good educator
in college is a complicated process: students enter college with a wide variety
of attitudes, values, expectations, academic and social skills, and assumptions
about the purpose of college, where and how learning occurs, and their roles as
learners. To use Terry Wildman's (2007) term, how do educators "nudge minds
to life" (p. 15)? Educators across a variety of positions (faculty, academic advi-
sors, student affairs staff) are expected to figure out how to respond to this
panoply of student characteristics, knowing that some of these characteristics
will change during a student's enrollment. To do either role well requires a lot
of effort, and being conscientious about the task at hand is often insufficient.

Furthermore, for educators to promote student progress, they need a clear
vision of educational goals, an understanding of the steps toward those goals,
and a way to assess student progress. In other words, they need to understand

and be able to assess students' learning and development. In this chapter, we set the stage for addressing this goal.

A strong assumption underlying the work presented in this monograph is that learning and development occur both within the individual and in context. Although different disciplinary perspectives or individual scholars' works may reflect a primary focus on development of persons (for example, psychology) or on characteristics of specific contexts (for example, sociology), we assert that understanding and assessing student learning in the context of higher education requires attention to learner characteristics and to situational or contextual characteristics, not one or the other. Just as there are many dimensions and layers of student learning and development (for example, reasoning skills, a sense of self, attributes of citizenship), there are many dimensions and layers of context (for example, social, cultural, and physical). Classic, foundational works such as Nevitt Sanford's (1966) *Self and Society: Social Change and Individual Development* and David Hunt and Edmund Sullivan's (1974) BPE (behavior-person-environment) interactional model published in *Between Psychology and Education,* as well as more recent books, such as *Rousing Minds to Life: Teaching, Learning, and Schooling in Social Contexts* (Tharp and Gallimore, 1988), illustrate this principle in their titles: learning involves the development of individuals and occurs in context.

Part of the relevant context for this work stems from collegiate learning goals and desired learning outcomes. For example, learning to think critically and in a complex way about a wide range of issues is a common learning goal in higher education (American Association of Colleges and Universities, 2002; Keeling, 2004) that has endured over time and is prevalent across a range of institutions. Nevertheless, students have persistently underperformed on various measures of complex reasoning (Pascarella and Terenzini, 1991, 2005), and educators remain puzzled about how to address the problem. In *Academically Adrift: Limited Learning on College Campuses* (2011), Richard Arum and Josipa Roksa triggered a great deal of interest consistent with this trend; they reported that only about one-third of the twenty-three hundred college students attending twenty-four institutions demonstrated significant improvement in critical thinking or complex reasoning over four years of college. Ernest Pascarella, Charles Blaich, Georgianna Martin, and Jana Hanson (2011) replicated their study using quantitative data from the Wabash National Study of Liberal Arts Education (WNS); their analyses yielded comparable results. In addition, the Accrediting Council for Independent Colleges and Schools (2011b) recently released the results of a survey of employers who reported gaps between the stated importance and applicant performance "on every skill and hiring criteria tested." These skill sets "ranged from sense-making and novel and adaptive thinking to cross-cultural competency and computational thinking" (Accrediting Council for Independent Colleges and Schools, 2011a). Such studies are valuable for alerting both educators and the public to significant problems of college student learning.

Based on our work to date using the qualitative data from the WNS (Baxter Magolda, King, and Drobney, 2010; Baxter Magolda, King, Taylor, and Wakefield, 2012; King, Baxter Magolda, and Masse, 2011; Perez, Shim, King, and Baxter Magolda, 2011), one reason for this gap and for low gain scores on measures that require complex reasoning may be that students have yet to develop the meaning-making capacities that support complex reasoning and independent judgments. Without developing the capacity to understand and learn from one's experiences, students are at a loss to know how to make intentional choices about what to believe and how to act. Similarly, without a means to access and assess students' meaning making, researchers are at a disadvantage in deciding how to interpret their academic performance and other behaviors, and educators are at a disadvantage in translating findings into the design of programs and services.

In this chapter, we map out how the capacity for complex meaning making evolves from late adolescence to early adulthood and how this capacity is reflected in and undergirds how students make sense of their experiences. Readers who understand the role of meaning making will be better able to document its effects on educational outcomes and provide better information to decision makers about program effectiveness. Our collective scholarship on student development and assessment supports the idea that complex meaning making is a necessary but insufficient condition for achieving complex college learning outcomes. Thus, an increased ability to assess development of meaning making would contribute to educators' efforts to understand, document, and promote these learning outcomes. We turn next to an exploration of meaning making and its evolution, especially in collegiate contexts.

Meaning Making and Collegiate Learning Outcomes

What is required within the developing individual to achieve learning outcomes such as thinking critically, demonstrating intercultural competence when interacting with others, and making discerning judgments about moral and ethical issues? Each arguably requires being able to reflect on one's assumptions, compare them to others' assumptions and perspectives, discern patterns and anomalies, and apply methods of inquiry to one's approaches and one's critique of others' approaches. These are commonly included among the habits of mind associated with a college education, especially when referring to professional education (Accrediting Board for Engineering and Technology, 2012) and liberal education (American Association of Colleges and Universities, 2002).

These habits of mind serve as interpretive filters through which people come to understand their own and others' experiences. When interpreting or making sense of such experiences, one is actively engaged in meaning making, the term used in the constructive-developmental genre to reflect this interpretive process. Applied to college student learning and development, meaning making refers to the strategies students use to understand what and how they are learning; each strategy provides the perspective that guides how they make meaning (not the content of their belief or decision). This perspective is quite useful: it provides a way to discern and understand who does what in the educational process, such as the roles of educators, parents and peers, educational and professional standards of practice, and students' responsibilities as learners. It provides a way of weighing sources of information and insights (including texts, Web sites, professors, staff members, and peers) to decide what to believe. A meaning-making perspective can also be thought of as a way of making sense of the world, such as figuring out what to believe, who to be, and how to act: it provides a guide for determining what to pay attention to, whose advice to listen to, what can be gleaned from a positive or negative experience, and in general how to navigate complex environments, including college campuses. As this range of applications suggests, meaning making is not limited to instructional contexts; it takes place in many dimensions of life. Robert Kegan (1982, 1994) identified three major dimensions:

cognitive (How do I know?), intrapersonal (Who am I?), and interpersonal (How do I relate to others?). (Researchers refer to the cognitive dimension as cognitive or epistemological. We use Kegan's designation here; elsewhere in the monograph, we use *epistemological* when discussing the development of this dimension to be consistent with that research. For an extended discussion of the multiple uses of the terms *cognitive* and *epistemological,* see King, 2010.) In each dimension, people actively construct their perspectives by interpreting their experiences.

When observing clusters of meaning-making perspectives, it is possible to discern commonalities among guiding perspectives or ways of viewing experiences; such perspectives may be reflected in standards or rules of inquiry used in certain professions or disciplines, but also in perspectives about academic success common to first-year students, as well as in issues raised by seniors trying to identify capstone projects. Educators who observe such clusters of meaning-making perspectives often differentiate between perspectives that seem naive or simplistic and those that reflect more complex worldviews and offer a more sophisticated set of options for navigating complex contexts. The latter are more consistent with higher-order educational goals and the demands of more complex occupational, social, and civic environments. For example, Marcia Baxter Magolda (2004) has called for advancing these broader perspectives for a twenty-first-century education by promoting the meaning-making perspective of self-authorship, arguing that this is a critical component of educating for the development of more complex perspectives and mature capacities to navigate complex environments. From a self-authoring perspective, people define their beliefs and act using criteria that are internally rather than externally derived.

The Nature of Meaning Making: Constructivist-Developmental Assumptions

How does the capacity to achieve deep learning outcomes and mature across many dimensions of development unfold over time, especially in educational contexts? Fortunately, a great deal of helpful theorizing and research about college student development can be applied to this question. Key to understanding the evolution of developmental processes is familiarity with fundamental concepts and definitions. We provide a more detailed section on meaning making and the constructive-developmental tradition for readers who are not familiar with this literature; we do so based on our observation that it is primarily taught in psychology and in graduate student affairs programs but rarely in educational policy, administration, or general higher education programs. (For other summaries of these assumptions, see Baxter Magolda, 2009b; Boes, Baxter Magolda, and Buckley, 2010; Kegan, 1982; King, 2009; Perry, 1970).

Meaning Making

Many patterns of meaning making have been observed by those educating college students and by scholars studying college student development. Kegan (1982) explained that people make meaning in "the place where the event is privately composed, made sense of, the place where it actually *becomes* an event for that person" (p. 2). Thus, what is of paramount importance is not the event itself but how the person makes sense of his or her experience. Kegan explained:

> *Being a person is the activity of meaning-making. There is thus no feeling, no experience, no thought, no perception, independent of a meaning-making context in which it* becomes *a feeling, an experience, a thought, a perception, because we* are *the meaning-making context [p. 11].*

Constructivism

Following Jean Piaget and the constructive-developmental tradition, patterns of meaning making are often referred to as forms (Kegan, 2000) or structures (that is, they are constructed by individuals to guide their interpretive processes—hence, constructivism). The activity of meaning making and the meaning-making structures that guide this process are not directly visible but are inferred through the ways individuals structure their arguments through key elements they see as important, their rationale for a choice or decision made, or the basis for their guiding beliefs or approaches. In other words, meaning-making structures reflect how we think (such as an argument's structure) rather than what we think (its content). For example, two voters might endorse the same referendum outcome (content) but for different reasons (structure). One might focus solely on whether the referendum personally benefits her, while the other might focus on the benefits to the community regardless of whether he would personally benefit; each reflects a different way of framing the argument and basis for choosing how to vote. It is important to note here that understanding what people think or feel does not help us understand their meaning making and that understanding their form of meaning making does not help us understand what they think or feel. Jack Mezirow's (1997) observation that "habits of mind are more durable than points of view" (p. 6) points out that a belief (the content of a point of view) is more susceptible to change than is how one arrives at a point of view (its structure). The durability of meaning-making structures reflects their role in guiding interpretations and behavior, even when they contribute to unproductive patterns that lead to conflict or lack of success. Kegan and Lisa Lahey (2009) refer to this as "immunity to change."

Developmentalism

This concept portrays the activity of meaning making as a dynamic phenomenon in which forms of meaning making evolve over time to become increasingly complex. There are several key assumptions underlying developmentalism. First, in constructive-developmental theories, meaning-making structures are ordered from simple to complex to reflect observed changes associated with age and maturity. Unfortunately, developmental patterns have often been portrayed in steplike images, as though development is strictly linear and observed patterns are discrete and discontinuous rather than cyclical and continuous (see Schwartz and Fischer, 2006, for a critique of such metaphors). In describing development, consider trying to summarize a film of someone running up stairs. Which frames would you choose? Most frames would show the feet on different steps, in between steps, or skipping over a step; only a few frames would show a foot planted firmly on the step, and perhaps only the first frame would have both feet on the same step. A similar dilemma is posed when attempting to summarize the evolution from crawling to walking (first, unsteadily and with many falls) to running. Yet the majority of summaries of developmental models are portrayed as discrete steps (as though a child only crawls, then walks quite proficiently, then runs with a smooth, steady gait). In the model we describe in this monograph, we wish to more accurately reflect both theoretical assumptions about constructive developmentalism and our own empirical findings on development toward self-authorship by describing and portraying development as continuous and cyclical.

Second, as each meaning-making structure evolves, it incorporates yet also transforms the prior structure, with the more complex structure retaining the prior structure as an element of its more complex system. As individuals move out of one meaning-making structure, they are simultaneously moving into the next one and may retain some of each depending on the context. For example, some contexts, such as social relations, may make more sustained or difficult demands on one dimension of development over the others, such as identity. Thus, contextual demands contribute to differing pace or intensity of development across the three dimensions.

Third, meaning making develops through cycles of differentiation and integration. That is, as developmental capacities unfold, individuals are able to step back from a point of view or a familiar approach to solving problems and take it apart to separately examine its individual elements, perhaps choosing to discard elements that seem problematic or no longer fit, retain some elements that continue to be useful, and revise those that need to be changed in some way. As they do so, the structure itself no longer consists of one intact way of knowing; instead, it comprises elements. The integration step of putting the surviving elements back together creates a new structure. As individuals cycle through various phases of the developmental journey and realize that this way of knowing has its own limitations, they are motivated to step back from it, critique it, and then reassemble it into a revised way of knowing, perspective, or habit of mind.

Fourth, the evolution of meaning making is a gradual process with periods of transition and consolidation during which the structures reflect more stability. New experiences individuals have for which existing ways of making meaning do not work well trigger an internal conflict. Piaget used the term *disequilibrium* to describe the internal conflict that arises when an existing mental structure cannot assimilate a new experience. This conflict then triggers the cycle of differentiation and integration and the creation of a new structure. A key aspect of this developmental cycle is the interplay between transition (the process of differentiation) and consolidation (the process of integration). Although reports of internal conflicts such as Piaget described are plentiful, the mechanisms underlying developmental change, including the role of disequilibrium, are not yet well understood.

Our fifth point here addresses an assumption that has frequently been ascribed to the constructive-developmental tradition but is seldom claimed by constructive developmentalists: the evolution of meaning making unfolds smoothly and in a linear fashion. Importantly, abundant longitudinal developmental research (Abes, 2012; Abes and Jones, 2004; Abes and Kasch, 2007; Baxter Magolda, 2001b; King and Kitchener, 1994; Mentkowski and Associates, 2000; Perry, 1970; Rest, Narváez, Bebeau, and Thoma 1999; Torres, 2010; Torres and Hernandez, 2007) suggests that the course of development rarely unfolds smoothly in a continuous movement from one structure to the next. Rather, patterns of development over time are better characterized by shifting distributions of responses (King and Kitchener, 1994; Rest, 1979). William Perry's (1970) work is also notable for including alternatives to growth.

Research on the implications of emerging patterns clearly illustrates the value of looking between as well as within the major structures of meaning making. For example, one well-documented finding stemming from research on moral judgment development is that during periods of transition, there is a higher degree of stage mixture (that is, individuals draw from a variety of meaning-making structures) and there is a positive skew in their response patterns (Thoma and Rest, 1999; Walker and Taylor, 1991); by contrast, there is a lower degree of stage mixture (individuals use fewer meaning-making structures) during periods of consolidation.

Stephen Thoma, James Rest, and Mark Davison (1991) reported that those whose patterns are consolidated evidence a stronger relationship between judgment and action than do those in transition. Exploring this further, Thoma and Rest (1999) found that "individuals use moral concepts differently as they cycle through periods of consolidation and transition" (p. 323), and Imjoo

Hahn (1991) found that those in transition drew from a wider range of moral concepts than did those with consolidated patterns. Studies like these show the complications of attempting to map development, especially in light of evidence suggesting that individuals' meaning making swirls within and across meaning-making structures. It is as though they are at first tentatively trying them on to see how well they fit; whether they fit for a given topic, context, or cultural setting; and if they work better than approaches that have not worked so well in the past. In explaining variability in data on skill theory, Kurt Fischer (1980; Lamborn and Fischer, 1988) proposed that individuals can access a range of meaning-making levels. This developmental range extends from one's functional (everyday) to optimal (peak-performance) level. Summarizing this research, Patricia King and JoNes VanHecke (2006) write, "Under conditions of low support, students function less skillfully and perform at their functional level, which is adequate for their everyday functioning but does not demonstrate their full potential. When students receive high support, however, they can perform at their optimal level, demonstrating their best possible performance" (p. 13). Karen Kitchener, Cindy Lynch, Kurt Fischer, and Phillip Wood (1993) extended Fischer's analyses and applied them to the development of reflective thinking. They found that performance varies depending on the availability of support and feedback: where these are offered, individuals operate closer to their optimal rather than their functional level. This variability led Barry Kroll (1992) to suggest that educators should direct their efforts at a student's leading edge of development (the optimal level) rather than his or her typical ways of operating. Although the framing of development as something other than continuous and linear makes the assessment process more complicated, it is more consistent with the evidence on developmental patterns and their emergence over time.

As we attempt to describe the evolution of knowing and acknowledge the challenges it entails for both students and educators, it is important to point out what makes the hard work of development worthwhile. More complex structures offer individuals more options for responding, clearer reasons for their choices (for example, because they can be based on endorsed values, not only on others' expectations), and the capacity to identify more ways of adapting to different contexts. They show increasing capacity in "connective complexity"

(King, 2010, p. 182), that is, the ability to see relationships and make connections between and across facts, observations, ideas, values, interpretations, and conclusions in increasingly comprehensive ways (see King and VanHecke, 2006, and Schwartz and Fischer, 2006, for a more detailed discussion and examples). In these ways, the development of more complex meaning-making structures is adaptive. And depending on your point of view, it is either a happy coincidence or no coincidence at all that these adaptive capacities bear a remarkable similarity to the capacities that students need to achieve learning outcomes during college.

Self-Evolution and the Journey Toward Self-Authorship

Kegan's (1982, 1994) theory of self-evolution traces the emergence of increasingly complex forms of meaning making during adolescence and adulthood and is grounded in the constructivist-developmental assumptions we have described. The development of one of these forms is self-authorship, which is particularly useful to those seeking to understand the development of college students and those trying to promote the achievement of learning outcomes in college. This theory has two distinctive features that inform our understanding of these phenomena. First, Kegan approaches the description of human development holistically; thus the forms of meaning making explicated in his theory include multiple dimensions: knowledge (how one knows), identity (who one is), and relationships (how one relates with others). Accordingly, constructing the meaning of an experience involves all three dimensions simultaneously; collectively, they convey the complexity of the meaning-making process.

The second distinctive feature of Kegan's theory is that the core of his theory is the subject-object relationship and how this changes as meaning-making structures evolve. Kegan's description is informative:

> *"Object" refers to those elements of our knowing or organizing that we can reflect on, handle, look at, be responsible for, relate to each other, take control of, internalize, assimilate, or otherwise operate upon. All*

these expressions suggest that the element of knowing is not the whole of us; it is distinct enough from us that we can do something with it. . . . "Subject" refers to those elements of our knowing or organizing that we are identified with, tied to, fused with, or embedded in. We have object; we are subject. We cannot be responsible for, in control of, or reflect upon that which is subject [1994, p. 32].

In each meaning-making structure, some elements are object and others are subject. It is the particular balance of which elements are object and which are subject that defines a meaning-making structure. As King and Ruby Siddiqui (2011) pointed out, there are several similarities between this aspect of self-authorship and theories of metacognition, or thinking about thinking. For example, scholars who encourage the development of metacognition (Kuhn and Dean, 2004) encourage students to be more aware of their metacognitive strategies; this requires that they have the developmental capacity to hold these strategies (how they think about thinking) as object.

Furthermore, although the subject-object balance underlying a meaning-making structure is fairly stable, it is not permanent, reflecting the periods of transition and consolidation we have described. The evolution to more complex meaning-making structures arises from elements that were formerly subject becoming object or moving what was unseen and unexamined to a place where it can be seen and examined. Kegan described this as the growth of the mind: "liberating ourselves from that in which we were embedded, making what was subject into object, so that we can 'have it' rather than 'be had' by it" (1994, p. 34). For example, in highlighting the distinction between two prevalent adult meaning-making structures, the socializing mind and the self-authoring mind, Kegan and Lahey (2009) focus on the movement of subject to object. In the socializing mind, people are subject to, and therefore shaped by, the expectations of their environment; they define themselves by alignment with that environment. In the self-authoring mind, they are "able to step back enough from the social environment to generate an internal 'seat of judgment' or personal authority that evaluates and makes choices about external expectations" (p. 17). Making the social environment object enables people to reflect and act on it—to "have" it rather than "be had" by it. Each successive structure thus reflects a rebalancing of what is subject and what is object, such that what was subject in one form becomes object in the next, and each structure incorporates, yet transforms, the prior structure.

The self-authorship literature itself has evolved, especially informed by Baxter Magolda's (1999, 2001b) work linking Kegan's (1982, 1994) theory to the study and promotion of college student development. She elaborated on the concept of self-evolution in general and self-authorship in particular as it applies to college students and strongly advocated for college educators to promote the development of the form of meaning making Kegan called self-authorship. With this capacity, one can be "the author (rather than merely the theater) of one's inner psychological life" (Kegan, 1994, p. 31). Students who let their issues trump their academic goals and ruin their relationships exemplify these theatrics. That is, students who are not yet able to author their inner psychological lives often allow external influences to derail their academic goals, jeopardize their identity development, or ruin their relationships.

Baxter Magolda (2008, 2009a) framed the development of self-authorship as extending along a continuum. At one end of the continuum are those who use a meaning-making structure with an external orientation. For these individuals, the source of beliefs, values, identity, and nature of social relations exists outside the individual in the external world. These individuals rely on external authorities (actual authority figures or societal expectations) to determine what to believe, how to see themselves, and how to construct social relations. Authorities' perspectives are accepted uncritically. Baxter Magolda used the term Following External Formulas to capture this external approach to meaning making. At the Self-Authoring end of the continuum are those who use a meaning-making structure with an internal orientation. For these individuals, the source of beliefs, values, identity, and nature of social relations exists inside the person in his or her internal psychological world rather than being dictated by those around him or her. The person reflects on, evaluates, and is an active agent in making choices about information from external sources to construct an internally defined belief system, identity, and way of relating to others. At the external end of the continuum, there is no sign of a meaningful internal voice. As the internal voice appears and grows, it moves closer to the foreground until it eventually comes front and center and the external voice moves to the background. When the internal voice sufficiently develops, it edges out the external voice. External influences do not disappear, of course; rather, these individuals use their internal voices to decide how to manage external influences. In between these ends is a form of meaning making that Baxter Magolda calls the "Crossroads," which reflects a mixture of external and internal orientations. People enter the Crossroads as they begin to question external authorities, work through the Crossroads as they process the tension between their emerging internal voices and external influence, and find their way out of the Crossroads when their internal voices have developed sufficient strength to coordinate external influence. This overarching continuum also emerged in Vasti Torres's longitudinal study of Latino/a collegians (Torres, 2010; Torres and Hernandez, 2007) and Elisa Abes's longitudinal study of lesbian collegians (Abes, 2012; Abes and Jones, 2004; Abes and Kasch, 2007). Jane Pizzolato's (2003, 2005, 2007b) studies of high-risk collegians also surfaced many of these meaning-making structures.

Returning to the discussion on the differences between the content and the structure of knowing, those who construct their knowledge, identity, and relationships using primarily external meaning making hold certain ideas and views. What is important developmentally is how they hold those ideas, in this case by depending uncritically on external sources. In contrast, those who self-author their knowledge, identity, and relationships may hold the same ideas and views, but they do so on the basis of internally generated criteria that coordinate their judgments of external influence.

In an interview about developing self-authorship, Kegan offered the following observations:

So [there are] two ways to be thinking about becoming more fully self-authoring. One way is that I am pretty fully self-authoring in some arenas of my living—say work—and I have sort of put some of these other arenas on hold because to maintain my self-authoring self in those is a higher art, a more complicated demand such as intimacy . . . there is some arena in which it is most easy for you to get the new structure together, then out of the comfort of that you risk applying it to other arenas—bringing along sides of yourself that haven't yet fully been reclaimed at the new more complex order of consciousness. . . . Another way you can think of becoming more fully self-authoring is the process of gradually exercising one's new structure from a more tentative to a more solid way of being, across all the arenas of one's living. For example, there may be a time when I have to use my self-authoring capacity largely to remain self-authoring. I use it to be on my guard for those situations where I might be likely to cave in again [Baxter Magolda, 2010, p. 278].

These comments reveal that a meaning-making structure may be more complex in one dimension than in another; for example, knowledge versus identity. They also reveal that a newly formed meaning-making structure may be more tentatively held than one that has had more time to become solidified.

Baxter Magolda's (2009a) twenty-five-year study of adults from ages eighteen to forty-three supports Kegan's perspective. She observed three elements within the Self-Authorship meaning-making structure: Trusting the Internal Voice, Building an Internal Foundation, and Securing Internal Commitments (Baxter Magolda, 2008). As participants developed a self-authored perspective, they focused on trusting their internal voices. As that trust increased, they turned to building an internal foundation, or philosophy of life, based on their internal voice. On occasion, they encountered contexts in which their trust faltered and they returned to develop it further as they continued work on the internal foundation. When they trusted themselves sufficiently to live the internal foundation rather than simply articulate it intellectually, they conveyed that they were securing their internal commitments. These three elements evolved in cyclical fashion over the course of participants' late thirties and early forties.

As this description of the journey toward self-authorship shows, it is complex. And just as a long voyage is simplified when only the major ports of call are listed, so a long developmental journey is simplified by noting only major phases of development. Similarly, just as a voyage seldom occurs without incident and in a straight path, a developmental journey also meanders as individuals interact with their environments and so can include both sprints and setbacks. Nevertheless, there are discernable milestones on the journey, despite obstacles and delays. It is in this spirit that we identify phases of development as milestones, and although we portray the milestones on a developmental continuum, we also assert that development across this continuum is better characterized as undulating, cyclical, or wavelike than linear, more like a swiveling helix than a fixed, straight line.

As we present the milestones and points of interest between them, remember that our purpose is to present the landmarks, not the journey between each landmark and the next (which might include forward strides, sideways shuffles, and meandering tangents). This is not a new idea. This is how Piaget (1948) set out the complexities of attempting to describe the evolution of meaning making in his stage model:

> *These stages must of course be taken for what they are worth. It is convenient for the purposes of exposition to divide the children in age-classes or stages, but the facts present themselves as a continuum which cannot be cut up into sections. This continuum, moreover, is not linear in character, and its general direction can only be observed by schematizing the material and ignoring the minor oscillations which render it infinitely complicated in detail [p. 17].*

In this monograph, we identify these milestones based on the theoretical work of Kegan (1982, 1994) and Baxter Magolda (2001b, 2008, 2009a), as well as the empirical findings from Baxter Magolda's longitudinal study (2001b, 2009a) and the qualitative longitudinal portion of the WNS. We have identified ten positions clustered into three major meaning-making structures: External meaning making, Crossroads (a mixture of external and internal), and Internal meaning making. Following Perry's (1970) rationale, we adopt the term *positions* for these milestones to indicate that they vary in duration, reflect key structures in use at particular times, and are "appropriate to the image of 'point of outlook' or 'position from which a person views his world'" (Perry, 1970, p. 48). Figure 1 (at the end of this chapter) portrays our vision of the development of meaning making in graphic form. We selected a helix to capture the circular rather than linear nature of development and to highlight the broad contours of development. This general trajectory of the development of meaning making from an external to an internal orientation reflects prior theory and research on the development of the complexity of meaning making. As with any other general trajectory, these broad developmental trends convey overall patterns, not individual variations. We attempted to capture the variability in developmental pathways through the use of interwoven strands of ribbons; these represent multiple possible pathways toward a self-authoring perspective.

Figure 1 also provides a brief summary of the ten positions on the continuum. Since a full description of each position is given in the following chapters along with illustrative verbatim excerpts, these summaries are offered here only as highlights. They should be read with an eye toward the underlying assumptions listed in this chapter and with the acknowledgment that more nuanced descriptions are provided elsewhere in this monograph. Based on our empirical findings, the three major structures are developmentally ordered, representing increasing complexity and adaptability. However, this order is offered without the expectation that these positions unfold in a strictly linear progression; instead, they are intended to capture the variations within the structure that are posited to occur through the process of transition and consolidation and that we observed in the data reported here.

Conclusion

As we noted at the beginning of this chapter, there are many challenges to gaining and providing a college education. In discussing leadership issues inherent in facing major challenges, Ronald Heifitz (1998) distinguished between technical and adaptive challenges. He argued that people cannot meet challenges requiring adaptation by simply applying learned skills; instead, they require a different mind-set with more sophisticated skills. This illustrates the importance of developing more complex meaning-making structures: they affect a wide variety of behaviors, such as whether and how individuals actively apply their knowledge to new problems in new contexts; whether individuals see themselves as problem solvers, innovators, or responsible community members; and in general, how they approach their work, relate to their family members, and live within their communities. These are high stakes and critically important for college students who are likely to serve in leadership roles in their occupations and communities.

FIGURE 1
Developmental Pathways Toward Self-Authorship

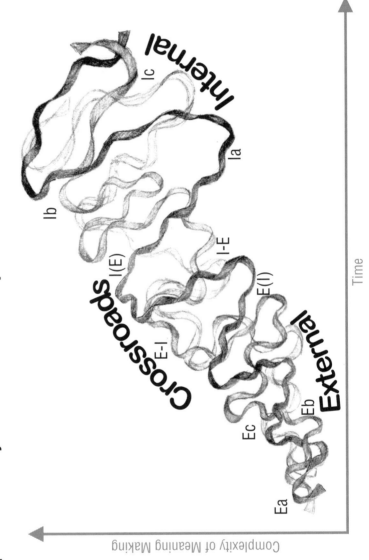

SOLELY EXTERNAL MEANING MAKING	CROSSROADS	SOLELY INTERNAL (SELF-AUTHORING) MEANING MAKING
Trusting External Authority (Ea): Consistently and unquestioningly rely on external sources *without recognizing* possible shortcomings of this approach.	**Entering the Crossroads** **Questioning External Authority [E(I)]:** Continue to rely on external sources despite *awareness of the need* for an internal voice. Realize the dilemma of external meaning making, yet are unsure how to proceed.	**Trusting the Internal Voice (Ia):** *Trust* the internal voice sufficiently to refine beliefs, values, identities and relationships. Use internal voice to shape reactions and manage external sources.
Tensions with Trusting External Authority (Eb): Consistently rely on external sources, but *experience tensions* in doing so, particularly if external sources conflict; look to authorities to resolve conflicts.	**Constructing the Internal Voice (E-I):** Begin to *actively work on constructing* a new way of making meaning yet "lean back" to earlier external positions. **Leaving the Crossroads** **Listening to the Internal Voice (I-E):** Begin to *listen carefully* to internal voice, which now edges out external sources. External sources still strong, making it hard to maintain the internal voice consistently.	**Building an Internal Foundation (Ib):** Trust internal voice sufficiently to craft commitments into a *philosophy of life* to guide how to react to external sources.
Recognizing Shortcomings of Trusting External Authority (Ec): Continue to rely on external sources but *recognize shortcomings* of this approach.	**Cultivating the Internal Voice [I(E)]:** Actively work to *cultivate* the internal voice, which now mediates most external sources. Consciously work to not slip back into former tendency to allow others' points of view to subsume own point of view.	**Securing Internal Commitments (Ic):** Solidify philosophy of life as the core *of one's being;* living it becomes second nature.

Source: Adapted from Baxter Magolda, King, Taylor, and Wakefield (2012). Reprinted with permission from the American College Personnel Association (ACPA), One Dupont Circle, NW at the Center for Higher Education, Washington, DC 20036.

Assessing Self-Authorship and Its Evolution

THE COMPLEX ASSUMPTIONS UNDERLYING constructive-developmental meaning making outlined in the previous chapter pose formidable challenges to assessing self-authorship and its evolution. This chapter draws out the implications of those assumptions for assessment, reviews the developmental assessment literature, presents current assessment processes, and discusses dilemmas in assessing self-authorship.

Assessment Challenges

Conceptualizing meaning making and self-authorship as a continuous and cyclical journey characterized by cycles of differentiation and integration, periods of transition and consolidation, variability across developmental dimensions, and multiple personal and environmental influences requires capturing these complexities in the assessment process. Among the major challenges of assessing self-authorship are accessing meaning-making structure, the intersections among structures, and personal and environmental factors that influence meaning making, such as the use of functional versus optimal meaning-making structures given different circumstances.

Structure Versus Content
The key challenge in assessing self-authorship and its evolution is accessing meaning-making structures. People tend to more readily express what they think than how they think about it or how they arrived at their perspectives. Effective assessment methods must get underneath the content of people's

---

beliefs, identities, and relationships to the core structures from which they make sense of their experiences. Kegan and colleagues suggested that topics such as anger, anxiety, and change produced subject-object information if the interviewee was able to reflect on these areas (Lahey and others, 1988). Perry (1970) asked interviewees what stood out for them, enabling them to identify rich experiences through which to discuss meaning making. Moral development research has used moral dilemmas to solicit meaning making (Gibbs and Widaman, 1982; Gilligan, 1982; Kohlberg, 1984; Rest, 1979). King and Kitchener (1994) posed ill-structured problems to entice interviewees to demonstrate their meaning-making structures.

Collectively, these scholars also emphasized respondents' reflections on their experiences, particularly in the form of reasoning or justification for their beliefs, identities, and relationships, in order to unearth the structure underneath the content. Researchers found that structure became apparent when respondents were asked to produce a response or actively construct meaning in response to some prompt. When respondents were asked to choose the better response from already existing responses provided to them (called a recognition task) they often expressed a preference for perspectives that they were not yet able to produce (Gibbs and Widaman, 1982; King, 1990; Rest, 1979). These dynamics led many researchers to use open-ended interview formats to solicit rich content, offer respondents an opportunity to produce a response and reflect on their reasoning, and provide a context in which the interviewer could help respondents clarify their reasoning, sharpen their arguments, and offer examples that in turn assisted the interviewer in understanding respondents' meaning making.

Relationships Among Meaning-Making Structures

Accessing the structure of meaning making is complicated by the gradual transformation of one structure into another, the incorporation of prior structures in newer ones, and the variability of use of structures across the cognitive, intrapersonal, and interpersonal dimensions of development. Kegan's commentary on ways to think about being more fully self-authoring (Baxter Magolda, 2010, quoted in the first chapter in this monograph) indicates that people might use a self-authoring structure in the cognitive domain but not in the interpersonal domain. They might also hold a self-authoring structure as a new, fragile meaning-making structure while still retaining part of an earlier structure, or they might hold the self-authoring structure fully. Kegan's portrayal is consistent with Rest's (1979) complex stage model of development, which suggests that meaning-making structures are usually not in full use at any given point and may ebb and flow in multiple ways. King and Kitchener (1994) reported that longitudinal data on Reflective Judgment supported the complex stage model. These variations make it challenging to interpret the mix of meaning-making structures a person holds at any given time; this mixture includes infrequent but observable use of more complex structures, or what Kroll (1992) called the leading edge of development. Kegan's Subject-Object Interview (SOI; Kegan and Lahey, 2009; Lahey and others, 1988) invites interviewees to discuss rich content across all three dimensions and in various contexts selected by the interviewee. The interviewer actively listens for indications of particular meaning-making structures, makes interpretations of the respondent's meaning-making structures during the interview, and asks probe questions to locate the limits of the person's meaning making to hone in on her or his meaning-making structures. Jennifer Berger's (2010) GrowthEdge Interview, an adaptation of the SOI to move beyond assessment to promote interviewees' development, uses this same process to identify a person's range of meaning-making structures as well as the center of gravity of his or her meaning making. Clearly these approaches require highly skilled interviewers who have in-depth knowledge of meaning-making structures.

Personal and Environmental Contexts

The role of context, both personal and environmental, complicates assessing meaning-making structures in general and self-authorship and its evolution in particular. Kegan (1982) argued that people *are* the context for meaning-making activity. Personal characteristics such as gender socialization, sexual orientation, faith orientation, race, and ethnicity mediate how people make sense of the experiences they encounter (Abes, Jones, and McEwen, 2007; Baxter Magolda, 2009a; Torres, 2010). Furthermore, socialization toward agency or communion yields stylistic preferences toward separation or connection within meaning-making structures (Baxter Magolda, 1992; Belenky, Clinchy,

Goldberger, and Tarule, 1986; Gilligan, 1982; Jordan, 1997; Kegan, 1994). Kegan (1994) noted how these have often been confused with meaning-making structures and offered a conceptualization of separate and connected forms of self-authoring in which meaning-making structure, rather than the style of the voice, identifies self-authoring capacities. These differences may be more likely to surface in open-ended conversations that allow people to generate important experiences and contexts, and with highly trained interviewers who can monitor their assumptions and explore further to discern interviewees' constructions of personal variables such as these styles.

These personal variations are intertwined with environmental variations that influence meaning making (Abes, Jones, and McEwen, 2007; Baxter Magolda, 2009a; Kegan, 1982, 1994; King, 2009; Pizzolato, 2003, 2010; Taylor, 2008; Torres, 2009). Kegan portrayed holding environments as "psychosocial environments that hold us (with which we are fused) and which let go of us (from which we differentiate)" (1982, p. 116). He advocated holding environments that blend confirmation (supporting individuals' current meaning making), contradiction (challenging individuals' current meaning making), and continuity (staying with individuals as they transition to a new meaning-making structure). A balance of challenge and support promotes development (Baxter Magolda, 2004; King and Kitchener, 1994; Perry, 1970; Piaget, 1950; Sanford, 1962), whereas an imbalance can stifle growth. For example, Pizzolato (2003, 2004, 2005) reported that privilege yielded insufficient challenge for growth, whereas marginalization yielded movement toward self-authorship out of necessity. Torres (2009; Torres and Baxter Magolda, 2004; Torres and Hernandez, 2007) found that dealing with racism had potential to initiate movement toward self-authorship. Similarly, Abes and Kasch (2007) reported that oppression based on sexual orientation created a context for more complex meaning making. Effective assessment needs to access individuals' holding environments and how they construct these experiences. Berger (2010) emphasizes this approach by exploring the way in which interviewees hold a structure in particular contexts.

King and Kitchener (2004) show how Fischer's (1980; Lamborn and Fischer, 1988) concept of developmental range (introduced in the previous chapter) addresses the interplay of personal and environmental context in meaning making. Translating Fischer's notion that people operate in a range from functional to optimal levels to the assessment of self-authorship suggests that an effective assessment needs to explore the conditions under which particular meaning-making structures are used and whether they reflect functional or optimal levels. The same holds true for the assessment process: if the process provides high support for people's reflections, it may yield their optimal meaning-making structure rather than the one they use every day, adding yet another wrinkle to the assessment process. Participants in the Wabash National Study (WNS; Baxter Magolda and King, 2007) and Baxter Magolda's (2001b) longitudinal study routinely reported that the interview conversation helped them reflect more deeply on their beliefs, relationships, decisions, and sometimes even life directions. As Baxter Magolda and King (2007) and Berger (2010) pointed out, self-authorship assessment interviews can be developmental interventions because they support sustained reflection.

Assessment Formats

The challenges posed by the nature of meaning-making structures have led many researchers to rely on open-ended interviews to access how people construct meaning of their experience and the conditions in which they do so. These interviews require highly trained interviewers to build sufficient rapport with interviewees, create the conversation as rich material emerges, explore interviewees' reasoning to identify structure, and probe for the edges of meaning making in all three dimensions. Highly trained interpreters are also needed to understand self-evolution sufficiently to hear and interpret meaning making and appropriately manage their own biases in this subjective process.

Because this process is time-consuming and labor intensive and because some researchers believe an array of approaches may better access meaning making, significant effort has been devoted to developing paper-and-pencil measures. Although not explicitly aimed at assessing self-authorship, efforts in moral and epistemological development highlight similar assessment challenges. John Gibbs and Keith Widaman (1982) translated Lawrence Kohlberg's Moral Judgment Interview (MJI) into a short-essay questionnaire, the

Sociomoral Reflection Measure, that retained the requirement for respondents to produce their responses and emphasized their reasoning or justification for their responses. The Sociomoral Reflection Objective Measure went a step further in providing reasons (linked to Kohlberg's moral judgment stages) from which respondents selected those closest to their reasoning (Gibbs and others, 1984). These measures correlated reasonably with the Moral Judgment Interview (Gibbs and others, 1984). Fully aware of the pitfalls of objective approaches that provide prototypical statements to respondents, Rest observed, "Some of the difficulties in using prototypic stage statements (justifications for a course of action) could be ameliorated by using issue statements (different questions that pose different ways of construing the most important problem in a dilemma)" (1979, p. 90). Rest developed the Defining Issues Test as a way to assess the development of moral judgment through how people understood moral dilemmas (most notably, whether they used moral principles to discern what aspects they saw as important). Also, consistent with his complex stage model perspective, he devised the scoring of the Defining Issues Test to allow researchers to assess respondents' use of multiple moral stages in evaluating these dilemmas. Thoma's (2002) synthesis of the major phases of Rest and his colleagues' research program reports the development of the Defining Issues Test, the emergence of Rest's four-component model of moral development, and the success of the Defining Issues Test in assessing the complexity of moral judgments.

Researchers studying epistemological development also devised paper-and-pencil measures. Baxter Magolda modeled the Measure of Epistemological Reflection on the format of the Sociomoral Reflection Measure and the focus of Perry's (1970) interview, yielding a short-essay questionnaire to assess the epistemological dimension that correlated well with epistemological interviews (Baxter Magolda, 1987, 2001a; Baxter Magolda and Porterfield, 1985, 1988). Wood, Kitchener, and Laura Jensen (2002) summarize extensive efforts to develop paper-and-pencil measures of epistemic cognition patterned after the Reflective Judgment Interview. They report explorations of written essays, a format that asked respondents to select from among paragraphs those that most closely matched their views, and the Reasoning about Current Issues test (RCI) patterned after Rest's Defining Issues Test format. Disappointed with the results, Wood, Kitchener, and Jensen wrote, "We no longer feel we can produce an 'objectively scorable' version of the Reflective Judgment Interview" (2002, p. 289). However, research on a computer-administered measure of Reflective Judgment (reflectivejudgment.org) is currently underway and shows promise for measuring reflective thinking. William Moore's (1989) Learning Environment Preferences, developed from Lee Knefelkamp's (1974) and Carole Widick's (1975) production task measure, translated reasoning from the Perry scheme to recognition items to assess intellectual reasoning, asking respondents to express their level of agreement with prototypical statements and then rank those that best reflected their perspectives.

Explicit efforts to construct paper-and-pencil measures of self-authorship are relatively recent. Pizzolato's (2007a) twenty-four-item Self-Authorship Survey, created by translating the three developmental dimensions into skill sets such as problem solving and autonomy, invites respondents to indicate their level of agreement with how statements reflect their typical ways of thinking and acting. Pizzolato (2010) noted the challenge posed by the fact that some items can be similarly endorsed by respondents at different phases of self-evolution and concluded that "qualitative methods may seem like the best option for self-authorship research" (p. 201), assuming that interview approaches invite participants to discuss meaning making in ways that illuminate cross-cultural variations. Elizabeth Creamer and Anne Laughlin (2005) and Laughlin and Creamer (2007) found that their self-authorship questionnaire provided information about whom students consulted for career decisions rather than how they constructed their consultations, the latter information emerging in interviews. Aware of the assessment challenges recounted here and in the interest of providing a psychometrically sound measure for assessing educational practice to promote self-authorship, Creamer continued work on the Career Decision Making Survey, which includes Likert-type items keyed to External Formulas, Crossroads, and early Self-Authoring (Creamer, Baxter Magolda, and Yue, 2010). Using the survey with college juniors and seniors resulted in eighteen items that show promise for assessing the three developmental dimensions, the three early developmental phases, and a matrix summary that portrays a range of meaning making (Creamer, Baxter Magolda, and Yue, 2010). Additional efforts to develop paper-and-pencil measures of self-authorship have been inconclusive to date (Goodman and Seifert, 2009; Pizzolato and Chaudhari, 2009).

For the reasons we have noted, our overall assessment goal was to access and then assess students' meaning-making structures; the mix of structures in use in various contexts; the intersections of cognitive, intrapersonal, and interpersonal dimensions; and the personal and environmental influences on self-authorship development. This led us to use in-depth interview approaches in the two studies on which this monograph is based.

Four Interviews to Assess Self-Authorship

Four interview protocols are currently in use to assess self-authorship. Kegan's SOI (Kegan and Lahey, 2009; Lahey and others, 1988) is the original interview constructed to assess self-evolution, including self-authorship. Berger's (2010) GrowthEdge Interview is an adaptation of the SOI that Berger uses as a developmental tool in coaching professionals. Baxter Magolda's (2001b) Self-Authorship Interview emerged over the course of her twenty-five-year longitudinal study of young adults ages eighteen to forty-three. The WNS Interview (Baxter Magolda and King, 2007) assessed self-authorship in a four-year longitudinal study of college students. Each of these approaches addresses the assessment challenges we have outlined to account for the features and nuances of self-authorship development.

Kegan's Subject-Object Interview

Building on Kegan's discovery of the type of content that encourages respondents to generate subject-object information and the need for reflection on that content, Kegan and colleagues devised a set of ten index cards to assist respondents in producing rich material for the interview that would help illustrate their meaning making (Lahey and others, 1988). The cards contain these words: *angry, anxious/nervous, success, strong stand/conviction, sad, torn, moved/touched, lost something/farewells, change,* and *important.* The cards offer respondents the opportunity to jot down notes about what these words bring to mind for them, helping them get in touch with reflections about particular experiences. They are then invited to start the interview by talking about a card of their choice. As they share their experience, the interviewer probes for how they are constructing their thinking, feeling, and social relating relative to the experience under discussion. As the conversation ensues, the interviewer generates possible interpretations of the respondent's meaning-making structures and asks probe questions to hone those interpretations. Probe questions attempt to learn what might have changed the experience for the interviewee, what was the most significant or difficult about an experience, what was at stake for the person, how the person came to her or his evaluation of the experience, or what a desired outcome might have been. The interviewer uses these types of questions to understand what interviewees take responsibility for, whose perspectives they can take or whose they are stuck in, and what assumptions shape their world views (Berger, 2010).

Lahey and others (1988) emphasize that the content of the conversation (that is, which cards are discussed) is less important than the respondent's ability to reflect on his or her experiences in ways that reveal subject-object relations. This interview maximizes interviewees' opportunities to express their meaning making in contexts of their own choosing. It requires highly trained interviewers to actively listen for subject-object information, generate possible interpretations to guide probe questions as the interview unfolds, and build probe questions throughout the interview to solicit the best data for interpreting meaning-making structures. The combination of interpreting and probing at the same time is a complex task. Trained interpreters score the SOI using an extensive training manual (Lahey and others, 1988) that outlines ten gradations of meaning-making structures. These gradations account for four major meaning-making structures and transitions among them.

Berger's GrowthEdge Interview

Berger's (2010) GrowthEdge Interview is an adaptation of the SOI that shifts the focus from assessment for research purposes (understanding development) to assessment for the purpose of supporting development. Berger's extensive experience using the SOI in leadership coaching led her to conclude that the process of the interview helped interviewees reflect on and better understand their meaning making. She ascertained that this was in part because the SOI interviewer focuses so intently on trying to understand interviewees rather than to change their meaning making. In the interest of using the SOI to help her clients find their growing edges and develop further, Berger renamed the interview the GrowthEdge Interview to highlight its differences from the SOI. Those differences are primarily in how she probes during the interview and her sharing of a report of the interview with the interviewee.

Two characteristics distinguish the GrowthEdge Interview from the SOI. First, Berger (2010) emphasizes probing for the range of meaning-making structures that interviewees demonstrate in the interview, as well as what she calls the center of gravity of their meaning making. These offer interviewees a more complete picture of their meaning making and potential contradictions they may be experiencing. Second, although she maintains the focus on structure, she pays additional attention to content in order to "understand the way the structure was held by this person and the content areas where I could see some developmental patterns cohering over time" (p. 256). These characteristics yield a report Berger shares with the interviewee in which multiple meaning-making structures and their interconnections are explored, as well as how they play out in various contexts. The complexity is captured in this example:

> In this dynamic space around the self-authored form of mind, people can be both pushing to close down their boundaries with others and also to open them up. Their trailing edges toward the socialized mind [Kegan's third order of consciousness] can lead them toward defending their boundaries with others and appearing as closed at times to other opinions and perspectives. Their leading edges toward the self-transforming mind can lead them toward loosening their boundaries and appearing as very open. Sometimes they express these distinct ways with different sets of people in their lives (as they are defended at work and opening with friends, for example) but sometimes they express these distinct ways with the same group at different times [p. 257].

These dynamics support the complex stage view of development; surfacing these dynamics enables the interviewer to gain a more nuanced view of the respondent's meaning-making structures. As is the case with the SOI, this interview requires highly trained interviewers. Berger also pointed out that the GrowthEdge Interview takes the form of a partnership between interviewer and interviewee and that this collaboration helps both partners gain a greater understanding of the interviewee's development.

Baxter Magolda's Self-Authorship Interview

This interview emerged as an adaptation of Baxter Magolda's (1992) Epistemological Reflection Interview that guided the college phase of her longitudinal study of young adults' learning and development. The college phase interview was modeled after Perry's (1970) opening question of what students identified as most significant and contained probe questions around areas that epistemological research identified as relevant to epistemic assumptions such as decision making, assumptions about teaching and learning, and how conflicts of opinion were handled. As Baxter Magolda followed 70 of her original 101 participants into a postcollege phase, they expressed interest in discussing not only their learning but also their thinking about themselves and their relationships with others. This led to broadening the interview focus and loosening the interview conversation to maximize participants' ability to express their meaning making.

The resulting Self-Authorship Interview (Baxter Magolda, 2001b) is an informal conversation (Patton, 2001) that begins with participants' reflection on significant experiences that have occurred since the prior year's interview. As is the case with the SOI, the content of the conversation is less important than the meaning the respondents make of their experience. As a result, Baxter Magolda uses probe questions to solicit a description of the experiences participants offer, how participants made sense of these, and how they were affected by the experiences. She uses probes such as, "Tell me more about how that felt for you," and, "Why do you think you reacted that way?" to unearth the reasoning for participants' thinking, feeling, and social relating. Probes such as "What was the best/worst about that?" help locate the edges or boundaries of participants' meaning making. Participants freely offer numerous experiences over the course of the approximately ninety-minute interview, often focused on the demands they encounter in their work and personal lives and how they approach those. In cases in which participants focus heavily on one developmental dimension, the interviewer asks questions to elicit experiences in the other dimensions. Near the end of the conversation, the interviewer invites participants to add anything else that comes to mind or offer their perspective on any changes they have observed in themselves. Baxter Magolda uses grounded theory methods and theme analysis to identify developmental patterns and assess self-evolution (see 2001b, 2009a, for an extensive discussion of this process).

Because Baxter Magolda has interviewed these same participants over twenty-five years (thirty participants remain in the study in the twenty-fifth year), an interviewer-interviewee partnership has emerged. Participants are familiar with the nature of the study and the interview. Rapport is strongly based on prolonged engagement and respect for participants' privacy. This rapport enables meaningful conversation that moves beyond the surface, as participants are willing to openly explore their own meaning making. Because the participants direct the nature and substance of the interview, the contexts that are most meaningful to them frame the conversation. Longitudinal interviews over such an extended period also surface personal and environmental contextual influences, as well as patterns of movement in meaning making over time. Similar to Berger's participants, Baxter Magolda's participants often comment on how helpful the interview is to reflecting on and further developing their meaning making. Their comments reveal that participating in the longitudinal study has influenced their self-evolution (Baxter Magolda, 2001b, 2009a).

Wabash National Study Interview

Using Baxter Magolda's Self-Authorship Interview as a foundation, Baxter Magolda and King (2007) crafted an interview for the WNS. The WNS sample included students from six institutions of various types and geographical locations, as well as students from diverse racial and ethnic backgrounds (Baxter Magolda, King, Taylor, and Wakefield, 2012). The WNS interview served two purposes: to assess students' progress on seven liberal arts outcomes and on their journey toward self-authorship. Taking the challenges to assessing self-authorship into account, Baxter Magolda and King designed the WNS interview to identify personal and environmental characteristics; identify the educational experiences students perceived as significant and how they made meaning of those experiences; and examine the intersections of cognitive, intrapersonal, and interpersonal development. They assumed that students' entering characteristics (including their meaning-making structures) mediated the experiences in which they engaged and the ways they engaged in them, and that in turn influenced how they made meaning of experiences to construct their views of knowledge, self, and social relations.

The WNS interview consists of three segments, each of which is constructed in situ, that is, as the conversation unfolds. In the opening segment, which usually takes approximately fifteen minutes, interviewers invite respondents to share any background information they feel is important, their expectations going into the particular college year, and the extent to which those expectations match their experience to date. Prompts solicit meaning-making clues as the opportunity arises. The second, and primary, segment (approximately an hour) delves into experiences respondents identify as meaningful. The broad "tell me about your most significant experiences" question affords respondents the freedom to choose contexts and topics that are most meaningful to them. The interviewer uses a consistent framework throughout the interview that invites respondents to describe an experience, how they made sense of the experience, and how it affected the way they decide what to believe, how they view themselves, and how to construct relations with others. To assist respondents in generating rich experiences and helping them to reflect on those, the interview protocol contains numerous possible questions that are introduced as needed to sustain a meaningful conversation. These include questions about respondents' "best or worst experiences, challenges or dilemmas they encountered, situations in which they were unsure of what was right, their support systems, conflicts or pressures they encountered, and interactions with people who differ from them" (Baxter Magolda and King, 2007, p. 501). These possible prompts also invite reflection on all three developmental dimensions. This second segment is the primary source of meaning-making structures in the interview conversation.

A closing segment of approximately fifteen minutes invites respondents to synthesize their experiences and meaning making. After summarizing key points of the conversation, interviewers invite respondents to put together what they are taking away from the collective experiences they shared. Prompts to assist them as needed include "how their collective experiences have shaped what they believe, who they are and how they relate to others; what insights they are taking away from their collective experiences; what they gained from the past year; the implications or consequences of their insights from the past year; issues these experiences raise; and how this year's experience has helped them consider their hopes for the coming year" (Baxter Magolda and King, 2007, p. 501). The interviewer may not need any of these prompts if respondents readily synthesize their perspectives. Typically two or three of these prompts solicit a meaningful synthesis. Interviewers continue to probe for meaning-making structures in this segment.

The WNS interview meets the assessment challenges by incorporating personal and environmental factors, using an open-ended approach that enables respondents to choose meaningful contexts, probing for meaning making, and including all three developmental dimensions. The WNS research team used an inductive process (described in the next chapter) for the initial analysis of WNS interviews in an attempt to identify any new possibilities in meaning making that might stem from the diverse WNS sample. The research team initially interpreted transcripts using a broad continuum of three phases: external, mixed, and internal meaning making. This broad continuum evolved into the ten positions presented in the previous chapter; the process of identifying them is the subject of the next chapter.

Conclusion

The complex nature of meaning-making structures and their varied evolution make assessing self-authorship challenging. Time-intensive interviews requiring high interviewer skill and developmental knowledge to elicit meaningful data often deter educators from assessing self-authorship. However, our experience in the WNS demonstrates that it is possible to train a large team of interviewers and interpreters to assess self-authorship. This training approach enabled the WNS team to collect 924 interviews from 315 college students over four years.

In the following chapters, we share our training processes and experiences, as well as the refined portrayal of the journey toward self-authorship that emerged. Our primary purpose here is to assist others who wish to become more knowledgeable about or proficient in dealing with the complexities of assessing and promoting self-authorship.

Development of the Ten Positions in the Journey Toward Self-Authorship

T HIS CHAPTER DESCRIBES how the research methodology and methods in Baxter Magolda's twenty-five-year longitudinal study and the four-year longitudinal Wabash National Study of Liberal Arts Education (WNS) culminated in the identification of a detailed model of self-authorship development reflected in Figure 1. Using an inductive approach consistent with the constructive-developmental paradigm in both longitudinal studies yielded rich data sets from diverse participants from which to identify nuances in self-evolution in general and self-authorship in particular. Over one thousand interviews from Baxter Magolda's study and over nine hundred WNS interviews enable us to describe a detailed portrait of the evolution of meaning making during and after college. In this and subsequent chapters, we show how young adults' capacities become more complex and adaptive over time and describe the strategies we have developed to assess and document these changes. In this chapter, we describe our analytical processes, how they evolved over the course of the projects, and the training processes we used with the research team to conduct and analyze WNS interviews.

Baxter Magolda's Study

Baxter Magolda initiated a longitudinal study in 1986 to explore the role of gender in college students' epistemological development. (Due to the longitudinal nature of this study, the methods have been previously published in

---

James P. Barber served as coauthor of this chapter.

Baxter Magolda, 1992, 2001b, 2008, 2009a.) As a constructivist, Baxter Magolda used Perry's (1970) and Mary Belenky, Blythe Clinchy, Nancy Goldberger, and Jill Tarule's (1986) theories to inform the college phase of the study but an inductive approach to allow new possibilities to emerge from the interview data. Baxter Magolda's (1992) guiding assumptions frame ways of knowing and patterns within them as socially constructed, context bound, fluid, and not generalizable. Continuing this constructivist approach in the postcollege phase enabled Baxter Magolda (2001b) to shift the focus of the project to a holistic exploration of young adult development that expanded beyond the epistemological to include the intrapersonal and interpersonal dimensions. The informal conversational interview described in the previous chapter yielded in-depth narratives of all three dimensions over the course of participants' twenties, thirties, and forties that illuminate the possible forms of self-evolution and self-authorship.

Baxter Magolda interviewed 101 traditional-age students (51 women and 50 men) when they began college in 1986 at a midwestern public university. Seventy percent of their entering class ranked in the top 20 percent of their high school class. Their majors included all six divisions within the institution (arts and sciences, education, fine arts, interdisciplinary studies, business, engineering and applied sciences), and cocurricular involvement in college was high. Of the 70 participants continuing in the postcollege phase of the study, 21 pursued additional academic preparation after college graduation, including law school, seminary, medical school, and various graduate degrees. Their occupations included business, education, social service, ministry, and government work.

Attrition over the past fifteen years resulted in a sample of 30 participants, all of them white, by year 25. Of these 30, 2 were single, 1 was in a committed relationship, 26 were married, and 2 were divorced (one of whom had remarried). Of these 19 women and 11 men, 22 had children. Seventeen had been or were pursuing advanced education: 12 had received a master's degree in education, psychology, social work, business administration, or economics. One had completed seminary, 2 received law degrees, 1 completed medical school, and 1 completed a doctorate. The most prevalent occupations of these 30 participants were business (16) and education (9). Areas within business included sales in varied industries, financial work, public services, real estate, and marketing. Educators were primarily secondary school teachers and administrators; one was a college professor. The remaining participants were in social work, law, homemaking, and Christian ministry.

Both Baxter Magolda's constructivist approach and the partnership she developed over the course of the study with participants mediate data interpretation. Her constructivist approach led to using grounded theory methods (Charmaz, 2003, 2006) to analyze interview responses. Each year she reviewed transcriptions of the taped interviews to identify meaning-making units and then sorted the units into categories to allow themes and patterns to emerge from the data. She reread data for each participant across years to develop successively evolving interpretations and further develop patterns. The credibility of the themes and patterns was enhanced through both prolonged engagement to build trust and understanding and the use of member checking to ensure accuracy of interpretations. Two research partners joined Baxter Magolda to reread and analyze data from years 5 through 11 in light of the broadened focus on all three developmental dimensions in the postcollege data. Each prepared summaries of themes individually, followed by meetings in which they discussed and synthesized their perceptions. This use of multiple analysts helped mediate subjectivities and increase the adequacy of interpretations. Baxter Magolda negotiates interpretations with study participants as well, and they receive publications from the project; in cases where their stories are told extensively, they review those narratives prior to publication. Full involvement with participants has yielded rapport and understanding. Yet D. Jean Clandinin and F. Michael Connelly (2000) emphasized that researchers "must also step back and see their own stories in the inquiry, the stories of the participants, as well as the larger landscape on which they all live" (p. 81). Thus, Baxter Magolda brings her perspective to the interpretation yet simultaneously works to be true to participants' narratives, and from the two, she constructs a theoretical perspective.

Baxter Magolda's portrait of self-evolution and self-authorship (2001b, 2008, 2009a) enhances understanding developmental possibilities by virtue of following the same participants from college entrance to their early forties. The depth of the interviews, strengthened by prolonged engagement and the researcher-participant partnership, yielded a conceptualization of Following External Formulas, the Crossroads (including listening to and cultivating the internal voice), and three positions within Self-Authorship (Trusting the Internal Voice, Building an Internal Foundation, and Securing Internal Commitments) and informed the WNS team's development of positions of the journey toward self-authorship. Yet because Baxter Magolda's sample entered college in 1986, were predominantly white, and attended one institution, exploring self-evolution and self-authorship with a more contemporary and diverse sample was warranted.

Wabash National Study of Liberal Arts Education

The WNS offered an opportunity to explore the development of self-authorship in the context of specific learning environments and in relation to selected learning outcomes. Its inclusion of six varied institutional settings, a diverse population of students, and a large research team enabled us to identify additional nuances and possibilities for understanding college student development and the experiences that promote it. (For details on the overall study, go to http://www.liberalarts.wabash.edu/nationalstudy.)

The WNS was designed to discover the student experiences and underlying developmental capacities that affect growth toward seven liberal arts outcomes (King, Kendall Brown, Lindsay and VanHecke, 2007). Although the WNS is a mixed method study (see Seifert, Goodman, King, and Baxter Magolda, 2010, for additional details), we focus here on the qualitative interview portion of the WNS because it provided key data to inform our identification of the ten positions in the journey toward self-authorship.

Conceptual Foundation of the Qualitative Portion of the WNS

Incorporating the constructive-developmental tradition and self-authorship theory, our conceptual model (see Figure 2) that guided the construction of the WNS in-depth interview can also be used to conceptualize adult development in multiple contexts. (Due to the longitudinal nature of this study, portions of the conceptual foundation and methods have been previously published. See Baxter Magolda, King, Taylor, and Wakefield, 2012.) The model

FIGURE 2

Developmental Growth in Context: Recursive Relationships Between Experience and Meaning Making

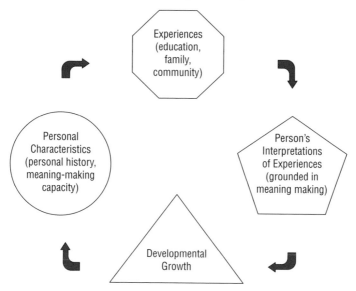

Source: Adapted from Figure 1 of Baxter Magolda, King, Taylor, and Perez (2008).

recognizes that students enter college with characteristics they have acquired from prior experience and that these inform the experiences they have during college. These characteristics include personal history (family structure, schooling, and health, for example) and ways of viewing the world, themselves, and social relations. This combination of personal and meaning-making characteristics mediates the experiences students choose in college, how they participate in chosen or required experiences, and what they learn from them. For example, an externally defined student whose family and faith community takes a strong stand against stem cell research might be reluctant to enroll in an embryology course that focuses on this topic. Should this student be required to take a course that includes consideration of this topic, she might enter it with some hesitation to consider multiple perspectives because they conflict with her prior learning and she might have difficulty demonstrating her mastery of the material. By contrast, another externally defined student whose family and faith community is supportive of stem cell research might seek out such a course and enter into it ready to entertain multiple perspectives but unsure of how to respond to those who disagree because she grounds her opinions in an external definition (here, the views of her parents) and has difficulty discussing the basis for the controversy. Students who are less externally defined are likely to be more open to learning about many topics, entertaining multiple perspectives, and engaging in diverse experiences regardless of the perspectives of others to whom they are close. Once students are in college, the college culture (including its subcultures) becomes a force that mediates how externally defined students choose and engage in experiences as well.

Students' meaning making also mediates how they interpret their curricular, cocurricular, and personal experiences. A firmly externally defined student might interpret the Socratic method as a way instructors make students learn content (or to avoid "real teaching"), whereas a student who recognizes the need to think critically might see it as a means to improve her critical-thinking skills. A student with little prior exposure to socioeconomic diversity might view those he meets in a service-learning project as exceptions to his stereotypes, might experience dissonance but not know how to respond, or might come away seeing the need to rethink his ideas. This last response is the one that potentially leads to growth on the liberal arts outcomes because it leads students to question or see the limitations of their current meaning-making structures; such growth requires varying degrees and types of support depending on the student's meaning-making structure as she or he begins college.

When students interpret an experience in a way that causes them to rethink and replace an earlier way of making meaning of the world, self, or social relations with a more complex way of making meaning, developmental growth occurs; this is the foundation for achieving key collegiate learning outcomes. Our recursive model suggests that as students adopt more complex meaning-making structures, they develop broader perspectives that enable them to make progress on the liberal arts outcomes and the three dimensions of development simultaneously. This growth then alters their "student characteristics," which in turn mediates future experiences.

WNS Qualitative Methods

WNS researchers used a two-step sampling strategy to select participating institutions. In the first step, nineteen institutions were selected from more than sixty colleges and universities responding to a national invitation to participate in the WNS based on their applications that described their vision of liberal arts education and the practices they implemented in the service of this educational goal. They were also selected to reflect a variety of institutional characteristics, including institutional type and control, size, and location. These institutions comprise the survey portion of the study. Students were randomly selected from among first-time, first-year, traditional-age students attending these institutions. In the second step, six colleges and universities were selected from the survey campuses to participate in the interview portion of the study as well. They were selected to yield a group of institutions that reflected different institutional types, a geographically diverse institutional sample, and student bodies that were sufficiently diverse to increase the likelihood of obtaining an adequate sample of students of color. The resulting interview campuses are four small colleges, one midsized university, and one large university; two are Hispanic-serving institutions, and one enrolls approximately 50 percent African American students.

Interview participants were selected from the students at six institutions who completed the quantitative survey component of the study who also indicated their willingness to be contacted to participate in an interview. Men and students of color were oversampled to obtain a more balanced distribution by gender and race/ethnicity. These steps yielded a sample of 315 students who were interviewed in fall 2006. These students were of traditional college age; 34 identified as African American, 29 as Hispanic, 27 as Asian/Pacific Islander, and 7 as being of mixed racial heritage. In addition, 11 identified themselves as international students and 2 more indicated they were born in countries other than the United States. Interviews were conducted on the students' campuses for the first three years; telephone interviews occurred in year 4. Of the original sample of 315, 228 (74 percent), 204 (64 percent), and 177 (56 percent) were interviewed again in the falls of 2007, 2008, and 2009, respectively. Participants received thirty dollars for each interview.

Interviewer Training

Because the interview protocol (described in the previous chapter) was complex, we developed a process to train a team of interviewers to collect the 924 interviews in the WNS data. Forty interviewers participated over the course of the longitudinal project, traveling in teams of three to six to conduct interviews on the six campuses for three of the four years; interviewers conducted telephone interviews in the fourth year due to budget constraints. Although members of the interview teams were located at institutions across the United States, we made efforts to bring the interviewers together for training whenever possible. This provided a consistent training experience across interviewers and also provided a context for discussion about best practices for interviewing. Interviewer training generally occurred annually over two days.

Interviewers were invited to participate based on experience as master's or doctoral students in higher education; therefore, all interviewers possessed at minimum a basic understanding of student development theory, higher education contexts, and educational research methods. The process for training interviewers is grounded in qualitative methodological literature. Prior to training, interviewers read a series of articles to add to their shared foundational knowledge of interviewing and provide a starting point for the in-person training sessions (including Baxter Magolda, 2004; Dunbar, Rodriguez, and Parker, 2003; Holstein and Gubrium, 2003; Kvale, 1996; Weiss, 1994).

Constructivist-developmental tradition asserts that biases cannot be separated from the interviewer; the best we can do is to identify and acknowledge our own subjectivities in order to better manage them in data collection and analysis. Therefore, following a discussion of the pretraining readings, training participants identified their own subjectivities about students, learning, the purposes of college, and so forth and discussed how these subjectivities might shape their interviewing. The process of reflecting on, writing down, and discussing our own subjectivities constituted the initial stage of our memo writing. In qualitative research, memo writing is a common technique for capturing thoughts and constructing meaning from the data throughout the data collection and analytical process. The memos written at each stage of the research (during training, immediately following each interview, during on-site interview team debriefing sessions, and throughout the summarizing process) are compiled for consideration as potential themes in the ongoing assessment process. Memo writing is a crucial element of grounded theory methodology (Charmaz, 2006) and was an ongoing activity over the course of the WNS.

Previously conducted interviews provided good food for thought, and reviewing them constituted a majority of our training time. To accommodate a variety of learning styles, training participants received transcripts for the sample clips so they could follow along the written words as they listened to the spoken exchange. Following each clip was an opportunity for discussion about what went well during the example and suggestions for improvement.

A central feature of training focused on distinguishing structure from content in these examples in order to train interviewers to recognize the difference and be better able in the moment to keep probing for meaning making. This differentiation of content and structure is one of the major challenges to assessing meaning making, and we devoted a great deal of attention to this topic in our training.

Interviewers listened to sample excerpts from previous interviews that were chosen to highlight particularly good examples, as well as situations that were challenging for interviewers. For example, one of our seasoned interviewers would often share a clip from his first practice interview several years earlier. During this conversation, the college student expressed a serious concern about the health of a former girlfriend, recounting his difficulty dealing with her eating disorder. The student became emotional during the interview, bordering on tears as he shared that each time he saw her on campus, he wondered if it would be the last time he would see her alive. This revelation was followed by eight seconds of silence and an abrupt shift to another line of inquiry. Although clearly not an exemplar of interview technique, the example illustrated to the training participants that all interviewers face difficult situations, and it opened the door to a discussion about more appropriate responses to a student disclosing personal information and expressing emotion. This example, and other clips representing challenging moments, reinforced to interviewers the often surprising willingness of students to share sensitive information with a complete stranger in the context of the WNS interview and allowed us to enter a discussion about intervention and referrals.

During training, we reinforced the importance of recording an interview commentary immediately following each interview. This three- to five-minute spoken commentary captured the interviewer's initial reaction to the interview and recorded key contextual information such as distractions in the area, student body language, and emotional reactions that otherwise would not be included in the interview transcript.

Following the formal training, participants conducted full practice interviews with undergraduate volunteers. New interviewers first observed an experienced interviewer, and a seasoned interviewer observed their practice interview. These practice sessions were audiorecorded. This served the double purpose of providing experience using the audiorecorder and allowed principal and seasoned interviewers to review the recordings for additional formative feedback.

Interview Analysis

Our theoretical framework and contemporary self-authorship research guided construction of the first data analysis protocol we used in the pilot study for the WNS (King and others, 2009). We constructed theoretical descriptions of meaning making at three developmental levels: meaning making based on external sources, such as societal expectations; meaning making that used a mix of external and internal sources; and meaning making based on internal sources, such as one's personally defined beliefs. We began with this broad continuum rather than specifically using any of the existing theoretical models because doing so provided a way to capture well-established general developmental distinctions that exist across several models and because existing research is not clear about the degree to which self-authorship reflects assumptions that are culturally specific. Because the WNS includes a diverse group of students, we used this approach to allow the particular details to emerge from the data. We initially used this broad continuum to interpret the 174 interviews from the pilot phase of the WNS (King and others, 2009). We used the themes in the pilot data to refine our descriptions of the three broad categories and used the second, refined analysis protocol described next to interpret the 315 interviews in the first year of the longitudinal WNS.

Analysis of the interviews took place in two phases: analysis of the content and analysis of the structure, that is, meaning making. The goal of summarizing is for the researcher to give her or his best read of the data presented through the transcript. Each of the two analytical phases resulted in a distinct summary; the Guide for creating summaries is discussed in the final chapter.

The Phase 1 summary identified important student background characteristics and experiences that the student identified as important to him or her, and the Phase 2 summary identified which of these experiences were developmentally effective (that is, which promoted more complex meaning making), and assessed the student's developmental level in terms of the three dimensions of self-authorship (cognitive, intrapersonal, interpersonal), and overall meaning making. The summaries were created separately, but each summarizing process began by reading the interview and the commentary to get a full sense of the narrative before beginning analysis.

Training for the data analysis process naturally built on the interviewer training we have described because most summarizers were also interviewers. Summarizer training was organized in much the same way as the interviewer training; meeting in person was deemed essential to provide an opportunity for sustained discussion about the assessment process. Ideally the same person who interviewed a student also created the summaries for the interview because the interviewers' insights from the interview interaction deepened their understanding of the participants' perspectives. This was not always logistically possible, but we made substantial efforts to retain interviewers as summarizers when possible. The interviewer commentary became particularly important when the summarizer of a transcript was not the interviewer. This commentary generally conveyed important information about body language, emotion, and so on, and captured initial reactions about possible developmentally effective experiences and developmental position. Because the time between interview collection and summarizing varied, the commentary also was helpful even when the same person was both interviewer and summarizer. The commentary was a critical component of the overall memo-writing process in the WNS, which also included the notes from daily interviewer debriefing sessions on-site during data collection and the detailed rationale included within the summaries for Phases 1 and 2.

The training process began with a set of common readings focused on developmental assessment and meaning making (including Baxter Magolda, 2008; Baxter Magolda, King, Taylor, and Perez, 2008; Ignelzi, 2000; King and others, 2009; Taylor, 2008). Training for Phase 1 summarizing focused on the nature and content of the experiences that students identified as important during the interview. The summarizers' task was to identify and describe these experiences, code the nature of the experience, and provide relevant excerpts to illustrate the student's description of each experience. Summarizers also identified which of the seven WNS liberal arts outcomes (if any) were reflected in the students' important experiences. We used student language whenever possible to capture as much of the individual's voice in the summary as we could.

Training for Phase 2 summarizing required a greater understanding of assessment and a clear grasp of developmental theory, in particular self-evolution and self-authorship. Summarizing also required balancing knowledge of existing theories with our inductive approach to identifying external, mixed, and internal meaning making, which we chose to enable new theoretical possibilities to emerge from the data. In Phase 2 summarizing, it is critical to differentiate content from structure. This is particularly difficult when participants use language that sounds internal when their meaning making is actually external. For example, a student who offers a reasonable rationale for supporting (or not supporting) stem cell research sounds internally defined unless it becomes clear that the rationale is an external formula that the student has not analyzed and cannot discuss in depth. Phase 2 summarizing also requires identifying when participants exhibit two distinct self-authorship positions at different points in the same interview. The interviewer commentary was crucial in providing additional insight that might help sort out these complex interpretations. As with interviewer training, continuing summarizers identified examples from their previous interviews to illustrate various gradations of development. The ensuing discussions constituted the majority of our time together in summarizer training.

Evolution of the Self-Authorship Assessment Guide
Throughout the first-year coding process, we became increasingly aware that our existing categories did not allow us to capture finer gradations in complexity

of meaning making that we were seeing in the interview responses coded as external or mixed. As team members discussed coding decisions, we were able to identify distinctions within the external and mixed structures. In attempting to identify and systematically code these distinctions in a way that retained the holistic attributes of self-authorship theory, we drew predominantly from recent research that explicitly addressed all three dimensions of development (Baxter Magolda, 2001b; King and Baxter Magolda, 2005; Torres and Hernandez, 2007). We sought to retain a holistic approach to meaning making by continuing to code for each dimension as well as assigning an overall level that captured all three dimensions. As our conceptualization of the meaning-making continuum developed, we were able to identify the three positions within external meaning making and the four positions in mixed meaning making noted in Figure 1. We used this more precise continuum to assess the 228 transcripts from year 2 and to reassess the year 1 transcripts.

Our annual coding and subsequent discussions of the data contributed to refining the positions; we edited the Self-Authorship Assessment Guide to account for these refinements as they emerged from the data analysis. Because we did not have extensive data prior to year 4 in the internal category, we relied on Baxter Magolda's three positions of self-authorship from her longitudinal study for distinctions in this phase. Thus, our theoretical framework and contemporary research grounded our initial interpretations of students' meaning making; subsequent analysis of these data led to an increasingly refined category system described in this monograph. Our process mirrors Perry's (1970) description of the evolution of his developmental positions.

Evolution of Summarizer Training

As the meaning-making categories extended from the original three groups into a more finely grained ten-position continuum, summarizer training changed as well. Just as the initial process of maintaining the external, mixed, and internal inductive scheme was difficult for summarizers familiar with Kegan's and Baxter Magolda's models, the shift to an elongated categorization was challenging for those accustomed to the three-category system.

The new system required a greater degree of focus and critical thinking on the part of the summarizers. The new system also called for a stronger constructivist

---

foundation and greater trust in the analytical skills of each individual. Whereas in the original system it could be very clear that a particular example illustrated an external form of meaning making, they now had the option of placing the same example into several external positions on the revised continuum. In this new situation, the principle of providing the best interpretation of the data took on elevated importance.

We therefore began to allocate more of our training time for reading and listening to interview excerpts and discussing as a group the meaning-making positions. We began to refine characteristics of each of the ten positions across the three domains of development and overall development. These refinements became essential for summarizers as they sought to interpret the complexities of meaning making.

Trustworthiness: Developmental Assessment

Our process for establishing the trustworthiness of the developmental assessments evolved as the assessment system became more complex. During year 2 analysis, many summarizers participated in an ongoing process of "workshopping" summaries during two seminar courses, each led by one of the principal investigators, as well as weekly research team meetings. Summarizers were asked to share with the other summarizers examples for which they were struggling to make an assessment. The group then engaged in conversation until they came to consensus about the developmental assessment. In this way, the research team developed trustworthiness throughout the process, complementing the initial summarizer training session. Over time we expanded and refined our understanding of the assessment through pooled judgment rather than relying solely on individual assessments.

The principal investigators continued to review approximately three summaries from each new summarizer throughout the course of the study; they also reviewed experienced summarizers' work on request. In addition, we conducted a thorough review of the year 2 self-authorship assessments that were interpreted as more than four positions beyond or two positions earlier than the year 1 assessment. We did so because this would indicate either dramatic growth or regression. Both are important and provided an opportunity to evaluate the quality of the assessments. Of 912 assessments, 132, or 14 percent, met the criteria for review. Of these, 83 (or 9 percent of the total assessments) were revised. This revision process revealed that identifying positions within the larger structures helped clarify distinctions among meaning-making structures and thus strengthened the quality of our assessments.

As we moved into year 3 assessment, we strengthened our summarizer training by sending each summarizer the same two interview transcripts before the training session and asking them to review and assign a developmental assessment for each dimension (cognitive, intrapersonal, interpersonal, and overall), identifying quotations from the transcripts to support the assessments. Then at the training session, we discussed our assessments, reconciled differences, and shared details about the process each used to arrive at the assessment. We continued peer reviews after training; experienced summarizers reviewed new members' initial summaries and provided feedback to ensure quality and consistency across summaries.

Nuances of Self-Authorship

The in-depth longitudinal interviews of both Baxter Magolda's study and the WNS form an extensive set of data for understanding the nuances of self-authorship. Together the two studies encompassed students who attended a diverse array of colleges and universities, represented different ages and generations of college students (from those in their early twenties, in the WNS, to their thirties in forties, in Baxter Magolda's study), and represented a diverse array of background characteristics, including differences in race and ethnicity. Both studies provided assessments that stretched from the beginning to the end (or near the end) of their time in college, and each provided an unusually large data set of four-year longitudinal interviews of college students. Although the size of the WNS research team constituted a challenge for training purposes and the logistics of data collection, it also enriched our analysis by virtue of providing multiple perspectives, subjectivities, and diverse sources of awareness about human development.

The nuanced portrait of self-authorship development that emerged from these two studies offers numerous possibilities regarding the complexity of cognitive, intrapersonal, and interpersonal development from the late teens to the early forties. The ten positions offer both researchers and educators greater insight into how students approach learning, their identities, and their social relations. These finer distinctions in students' meaning making are best understood through student narratives that trace their evolution over time. The next four chapters offer in-depth student narratives from both studies to illustrate these fine distinctions, their evolution, and the fluid, sometimes nonlinear trajectories of development.

Trusting External Authority: External Positions

THIS CHAPTER DESCRIBES THE THREE POSITIONS that make up the External meaning-making structure on the journey to a self-authoring meaning-making perspective (see Figure 1). Each of these early developmental positions reflects variations of externally defined meaning making. Each is illustrated with interview quotations that highlight the essence of each and the distinctions among the three.

At the initial levels of development, the predominant meaning-making structure reflects a firmly grounded external orientation, that is, the individual relies strongly on external sources for knowledge, self-definition, and decisions about how to relate socially. There is no indication of an internal voice guiding these decisions.

At the same time, there are differences in the degree to which individuals rely on an external orientation to make meaning of the world. That is, a person who makes meaning using an early external position (Trusting External Authority, [Ea]) consistently and unquestioningly relies on external sources without recognizing possible shortcomings of this approach. By contrast, an individual who operates from a middle external position (Tensions with Trusting External Authority, [Eb]) relies fairly consistently on external sources but may experience tensions in some areas in doing so, particularly if external sources conflict with each other (such as getting conflicting advice from two trusted friends); these individuals often look to authorities to resolve these conflicts. Finally, a person who operates from a late external position (Recognizing

---

Rosemary J. Perez served as coauthor of this chapter.

Shortcomings of Trusting External Authority, [Ec]) relies on external sources and recognizes that this stance has its shortcomings, but has not yet developed an internal voice to provide an alternative viewpoint. Thus, even within the late external orientation, these individuals still look to authorities for some process to resolve these shortcomings since they do not have an internal voice to draw on.

Trusting External Authority

Individuals whose approach is characterized as Trusting External Authority (Ea) consistently and unquestioningly rely on external sources to make meaning of their experiences. Cognitively they see knowledge in terms of right or wrong and as truths that only highly trained experts possess. These individuals also tend to follow formulas provided by authority figures for making life decisions; their underlying rationale here is that these should yield the "right" answer or at least a predictable result. When they confront ambiguity, they look to authority figures or authoritative sources to eliminate the ambiguity and provide the "right" answer. At this point, they lack trust in their own ability to discover an acceptable solution. In their intrapersonal development, individuals dependent on external influences base their identities almost exclusively on the beliefs and values with which they are most familiar and comfortable (for example, those from their childhood and adolescence) rather than those they have examined. They are often strongly committed to their values but cannot explain why they are important to them beyond having been raised that way. Ultimately they trust that others know them better than they know themselves. In the interpersonal realm, individuals who operate from the Trusting External Authority position tend to defer to others' ideas and opinions, especially in relationships where they see themselves as less qualified or experienced. They also seek to build relationships with others who are similar to them and may be hesitant to interact with those who are different. If conflict arises, they ignore or avoid the source of tension for the sake of keeping others happy. In sum, individuals who use the Trusting External Authority position show no recognition of possible shortcomings of this approach and thus are content with depending on others for their identity, relationships, and beliefs.

Gavin, a first-year engineering major at a midsized institution who participated in the WNS, illustrated the Trusting External Authority position during his year 1 interview. (All names are pseudonyms.) He had attended an all-male high school and the college from which his parents and brother had graduated. He reported worrying about failing in college and often second-guessed his decisions. Discussing his college selection process, Gavin explained:

> *My mom actually pointed me toward [this college]. . . . I hadn't even thought about it. I really didn't do much college research on my own, I mean, I read* The Princeton Review's *Best 367 or 357, whatever it was. I'd read that and go through that and I looked at some schools, I looked at some schools in Boston, but, my mom really, I mean even though she graduated from here, she really pointed me towards, I think she was kind of leaning towards [name of another college], she really thinks that I'm going to end up being an engineer so, that's really why she wanted to point me towards that. My dad pretty much pointed me towards [this college], just making the points of I'm going to meet a lot of great people here and everything, and he just thought it was a really important experience for me. And then my brother, just you know, all the way towards [this college], he headed me towards that.*

After hearing his family members' recommendations for which college to attend, Gavin considered several factors, including the amount of financial aid he would receive and the quality of student life at each institution. Ultimately he chose the institution his father and brother favored, in spite of the more attractive financial aid package he received from the school his mother favored. He explained:

> *When I started thinking about student life and the people I would meet here, the contacts I would make, the professors that I would have, the, the freedom to switch between whatever college I want because I know that I'm going to get a top quality education, that made it all worth the money to me.*

Although Gavin was able to articulate a rationale for the college he chose to attend, he did not demonstrate significant internal criteria and remained heavily dependent on others' expectations during his decision making. His comment that he did not do much research on colleges on his own indicates that he trusted others to know what was best for him and viewed his parents, as well as his older brother, as the primary sources of information. Furthermore, he did not acknowledge the conflicting advice he received from his mother compared with his father's and brother's advice. Not addressing or reconciling this may have been his way of avoiding conflicts, a topic he noted in a later interview.

Once Gavin entered college, he continued to trust others' ways of knowing over his own, even when doing so created challenges for him. For example, he explained how he approached his large lecture chemistry course:

> I can't understand my professor at all. He has these PowerPoint slides, and that's really helpful because I don't have to take notes and I can just access that at any time, but, he's up there talking about stuff and he goes into depth, like in depth. I mean he's a great researcher and everything, but I don't know how good of a teacher he is . . . I went to [a] review session; there was this student in there, he was a junior, and he explained it so much better because he knew what it was like to learn this stuff, so I learned more from him in two hours than I did in my chem class for four weeks.

Asked to elaborate on how he made sense of his experience at the review session compared with his experiences in class, Gavin stated:

> I was like, "Wow, why am I going to class if I can just download the notes and just go to these review sessions and figure it out for myself?" because essentially that's what I'm doing. And I don't know, I'm just going to keep going to class and stuff because I'm spending so much money to be here that I think it's important that I go to class and just get exposed to the subjects as much as I can.

While seeking out ways to better learn the course material, Gavin discovered approaches to learning that he found more effective than attending class.

Nonetheless, he diligently attended class because he was paying for it and with the assumption that he would somehow gain knowledge from the professor.

Interestingly, Gavin distinguished between the professor's abilities as a researcher and as a teacher. Through this distinction, he superficially reconciled the tension he experienced between seeing the professor as the expert and not understanding the information the professor provided. Gavin never questioned the professor's expertise and instead assumed that the professor simply struggled to express the ideas in terms that Gavin and his classmates could understand. Although Gavin described having to figure out chemistry on his own, he was clearly reliant on the older student to help him learn the material. Moreover, he avoided conflict by choosing not to approach the professor with his concerns but instead found other forums for learning the material.

Outside the classroom, Gavin also sought to avoid conflict—an attribute that is often motivated by a desire to please others. In sharing a roommate conflict in which his needs and those of his roommate clashed, he explained:

> Usually if I encounter a conflict, I just ignore it and then go find somebody else, or go talk to somebody else, or I can talk to other people about it. And, then if I'm having a huge problem, there's a lot of people here who I can talk to, I mean, there's a priest on our floor, and the rector said, "Any time you need to talk, talk to me." My RA's [resident advisor] a great guy; I can talk to him anytime.

Here again, Gavin looked to external sources such as the rector and the RA to share his feelings with them rather than address the issue with his roommate. Thus, the authority figures may help him resolve his feelings, which enables him to avoid, and therefore not resolve, conflict with his peers. By ignoring sources of disagreement or frustration, he consistently—though unconsciously—allowed others' needs and desires to take precedence over his own.

When Gavin encountered areas where no clear right or wrong answer existed, he expressed discomfort and worked to identify concrete rules for dealing with the ambiguity. For example, he described anthropology as "a whole different kind of thinking, which is really weird," and noted that the course challenged him to look at other people's ways of thinking:

It's more a thinking outside the box class to me; it's, "What have you been exposed to your whole life and now, step outside the box and evaluate what you've been exposed to," and be like, "Was that the right way?" and look at other people's way and, I'll be like, "That's the wrong way; this is how we do it." What is the right way?

In response to the interviewer's asking, "How do you decide what is the right way?" Gavin answered:

Well, I guess you just . . . you just exercise culture relativity and just . . . we hadn't really declared a right way, though. I mean, you can't, because unless you make a clear definition of what it's about in the whole, I guess the human life, I don't know, I guess whenever it promotes human life and what it would be, to me, that is what's important but, even that I can't make a clear definition because that's what matters to me as a Christian. To somebody else, it might be something completely different, like what's going to give them the most power.

The lack of a clear definition and set of values to guide the decision-making process frustrated Gavin. Although he understood the concept of cultural relativity, he struggled to apply it and had yet to see its shortcomings. At this point, he had not developed the confidence to think through a morally ambiguous situation without the guidance of an authority figure.

Throughout his year 1 interview, Gavin made meaning through Trusting External Authority. Because he is thoughtful by nature, he did not necessarily follow external formulas without question; however, the questions he tended to raise (for example, "Which college will give me the most for my money?" "How else can I learn chemistry?") suggested that he was looking for the right answer. In addition, he turned to authorities or external sources to find solutions to such questions. He exhibited the key characteristics of Trusting External Authority: assuming authorities had the answers, identifying himself through external expectations, and deferring to others in relationships.

Tensions with Trusting External Authority

Individuals who use the Tensions with Trusting External Authority (Eb) position consistently rely on external sources but experience tensions in some areas when they do so, especially when external sources conflict with each other. They prefer to follow external formulas and may follow different formulas in different contexts as a way to adapt to seeing (but not knowing how to integrate) multiple perspectives. Cognitively they begin to recognize that at least some areas of knowledge are subjective and open to interpretation; within these areas, they do not consistently or internally evaluate evidence. Their discomfort with ambiguity may result in shifting among multiple interpretations. Although they see the need to question and analyze information, they have not yet developed a set of criteria to do so. Intrapersonally, they continue to use social expectations to form and express their identity but acknowledge that their identity can shift and change. They find the process of defining their identity to be daunting and experience difficulty behaving consistently or in ways that allow them to acknowledge their own views and values; thus, they often continue to defer to others' expectations and perceptions. In the interpersonal dimension, individuals are willing to share their ideas when working with others but do so in order to gain approval or acceptance from others. Because they are so strongly concerned with how others perceive them, they seek to avoid conflict and maintain consensus. Also, individuals who make meaning from this position may demonstrate a budding curiosity about those who are different from them and begin to interact with a more diverse group of peers. Yet if they experience tension between two groups with competing needs or interests, they move between pleasing one group and pleasing the other. As a result, for individuals with this meaning-making structure, their identity and their priorities within relationships are not guided by a coherent sense of self and self-in-relationship but fluctuate depending on the time and place.

We return to Gavin's college experience since his predominant meaning-making position moved from Trusting External Authority (Ea) to Tensions with Trusting External Authority (Eb) in his year 2 interview; this demonstrates the subtle but significant distinctions between these two positions. During his second year of college, Gavin more fully recognized that subjectivity exists, but he still tried to maintain objectivity. Discussing how he formulates his own views, he stated:

> *I guess I try to look at everything objectively and [sighs] I guess, I don't know . . . I don't know. I guess just staying objective and looking for the best result while trying to consider all the factors.*

Gavin acknowledged that he was seeing "a lot of gray all the time," which made him uneasy. In light of his discomfort, he noted, "It's important for me to have mentor figures who I trust and who I believe in give me their opinions in terms of black and white instead of gray." While he recognized and accepted the uncertainty of knowledge during his year 2 interview, he nonetheless surrounded himself with mentors who could paint knowledge in more black-and-white terms so as to ease his anxiety with the shades of gray he was seeing. He also grappled with ambiguity by simply giving up on finding an answer to some issues, such as the war in Iraq. He explained:

> *I get in so many conversations with people talking about whether it's a just war or like good or bad or whether they're for it or against it and I've heard so many good points, but I've gone from being for it to against it to back in the middle, and so some things I just kind of give up on. I know that I'll never know everything about that situation. There's just no way and so I'm not going to pretend to make an opinion about it, so there's some things that I just try to leave alone.*

Gavin's opinion about the war in Iraq fluctuated based on his discussion with others. Lacking a consistent, internally grounded basis for his opinion and doubting his ability to gain sufficient knowledge to form an opinion, he chose to abandon his search for what he believes.

Because Gavin more fully recognized subjectivity in his sophomore year, he began to see both benefits and liabilities of having more than one right answer. He noted:

> *[Seeing shades of gray is] a strength in that it means that you're considering both sides of things, not just being one or the other. . . . It*

clarifies that you must have considered factors from both sides and that's a really important thing, but being black or white, that doesn't mean that you haven't considered both sides. And so being gray is a weakness because it's indecisive and you need to be decisive and make decisions all the time.

The pressure he felt to be decisive compelled Gavin to continue to find external formulas to follow. Ultimately he articulated the importance of questioning and analyzing information, but he still felt there should be a resolution of the shades of gray.

Gavin continued to focus on meeting his parents' and professors' expectations in his sophomore year. He believed there were significant costs associated with not having the right answer. Explaining why subjectivity drives him "up the wall," he stated:

Somebody one day could tell me one thing and then another, they could tell me another thing and they could both claim to be right . . . and I could spend my whole life trying to figure out who's right and what this guy meant and if I came to like [laughs], you know, I could arrive at the wrong conclusion. I mean spend my whole life analyzing something and having it ending up, be no right answer. . . . I feel like I wasted my time and [laughs] my efforts.

Asked to explain why he finds wasting his time and efforts problematic, Gavin added:

I mean I feel like I owe it to the people who have supported me and given their time and efforts into me—my teachers in high school and my parents and the people who are funding the scholarships for me to come to school here. I feel like I owe it to them to do something with my life.

Gavin's desire to live up to what he thought others expected of him fueled his quest for a right answer. He conveyed several key characteristics of Tensions with Trusting External Authority: discomfort with uncertainty, lack of clarity of his own perspective, and a sense of obligation to live up to others' expectations.

Recognizing Shortcomings of Trusting External Authority

Individuals whose approach is characterized as Recognizing Shortcomings of Trusting External Authority (Ec) still rely on external sources but recognize that this stance has shortcomings. However, they hesitate to take responsibility for making decisions about their identities, relationships, and beliefs because they have not yet figured out how to do this, including using internally grounded criteria. Instead they embrace an eclectic, sometimes conflicting set of beliefs and values from external sources. The individual's cognitive meaning making at this point is characterized by an increasing sense of comfort with seeing a broad span of knowledge as uncertain and based on one's particular background and vantage point. Individuals are able to appreciate multiple perspectives, and they begin to develop some criteria for evaluating such perspectives. Nonetheless, others still influence their perception of what constitutes valid ways of knowing. Intrapersonally, individuals who make meaning from this position are beginning to question and see the need to further explore aspects of who they are. They can recognize—but not yet mediate—the influence of others. At this point, they may feel lost and confused as they let go of an identity that others had defined for them and search for an alternative strategy. In the interpersonal dimension, individuals continue to seek others' approval and acceptance but may experience frustration when doing so. They are increasingly aware of when a relationship does not meet their needs or align with their beliefs and values; however, they still hesitate to consider their needs as equal to those of others. When interacting with those who are different, individuals at this position start to identify and explore both the similarities and differences that exist between themselves and others.

Sarah, a sophomore WNS participant double-majoring in art history and business, used the Recognizing Shortcomings of Trusting External Authority (Ec) meaning-making position during her sophomore-year interview. She is a first-generation college student whose parents are divorced. She not only saw shades of gray but also enjoyed thinking in ways that acknowledged the uncertainty inherent in interpretation:

Well, art history is [laughs] all about interpretation, so to a certain
extent, there's always one absolute interpretation, you know, the rea-
sons why and for historical purposes, but then there's always how
you feel about it and what you can see out of it, and that happens
more with contemporary art than classical. But, I mean everything's
up for interpretation, and it's kind of neat to hear all the sides, and
it's kind of neat to have the opportunity to just kind of BS your way
through a test [laughs] because it's, you know, you can do that.

This student distinguishes between the "one absolute interpretation" based
on reasons and historical purposes and the variety of ways different people can
feel about and see art. She is interested in the variety of opinions yet labels
them "BS" for testing purposes. She does, however, acknowledge greater uncertainty interpreting contemporary art. When asked if her interpretation ever
conflicted with someone else's, she offered this:

Always. Oh, yeah. Especially with the more contemporary art
because there is no one interpretation. Even the artist doesn't really
have an interpretation of what they're doing and so you could say some-
thing and say, "I feel this. Like I really think that this color . . . ," and
someone's like, "No, I think it's completely opposite." You're both
right. I mean it's just because the way that more contemporary
artists do their work is to make people interpret things differently,
so it's kind of the reaction that they're looking for.

In this context, Sarah believed that the artists were trying to get people to
have different reactions. Asked how she decided on her interpretation, she
added:

Well, I'll take the one that makes the most sense or I'll give my input
or I just, you know, it's usually just a less interesting view. You kind
of leave it to the people who own the view and you kind of take
yours for what you have and I guess cherish it [laughs].

Although Sarah does not clearly articulate how she comes to her perspective, she is now open to multiple perspectives and people owning their own views. Yet she considers her viewpoint as "less interesting" than those of authority figures (in this case, the artists themselves), suggesting that she has yet to own her personal view.

As Sarah grew more comfortable with multiple ways to interpret forms of art, she also recognized the importance of her own interpretation of her identity. In her first year, she reported volunteering to be the designated driver for her friends to avoid their pressuring her to drink at parties. By her second year, she reported the most important insight she had gained during her first year: "I guess being myself, not really trying to be good for everyone, is really important to me, and I think that's what I want." Describing what "being herself" meant to her, she stated:

> *I guess just admitting what I like rather than being around someone and they're saying, "I don't like this show," and you're like, "Me, neither." Like be like, "Well, I'm going to watch it and see what I feel," you know, and if we differ on it or what. . . . And just learning to put those kind of differences aside even, you know, to be a friend with someone or to be okay with someone, not necessarily adapting to exactly what they like, but just learning how to accept it and having them accept me for who I am or what I like or what I feel and that kind of thing, so that's kind of being myself [laughs].*

Sarah was working on relying less on others' perceptions of her becoming her true self and expressing her own opinions. She is less afraid of conflict and less focused on pleasing others; as a result, she is more willing, though still hesitant at times, to situate her own needs as equally important to those of others.

Sarah's emphasis on learning to accept others and have them accept her for who she is functioned as a precursor to developing mutual respect in relationships. In the interpersonal realm, she was trying to learn to balance doing things for herself and using her support systems. She reported that her mother was her best friend, yet Sarah evaluated when her mother was in a position to give her good advice:

It's kind of a 50/50 between my mom and my boyfriend. If I have an issue, I talk to one of them depending on what my issue is because I kind of know who would give the better advice in the situation. My mom's always given me good advice, but some stuff she wouldn't understand, you know, today's college stuff . . . so I talk to her about everything and I talk to my boyfriend about everything. And, so I mean they just help me if I'm sad or lonely.

Although Sarah still followed others' advice without weighing in herself, she now realizes that however well intentioned, her mother's advice has its shortcomings (in this example, that she doesn't understand "today's college stuff"). By questioning the basis for her mother's advice, she is acknowledging that it has its shortcomings (it is not complete). This realization allows her to expand her options when seeking advice to spread her dependencies among those she trusts.

Sarah's comments highlight the key characteristics of Recognizing Shortcomings of Trusting External Authority: an increasing openness to uncertainty, recognition of the need to be oneself, and an awareness of the potential conflict between one's own and other's expectations.

Developmental Progression in External Meaning Making

The characteristics of the three external meaning-making positions form a developmental progression toward increasingly complex meaning making. Examples of Trusting External Authority meaning making focused on acquiring absolute knowledge from authorities, defining identity through external expectations, and pleasing others in relationships. The primary distinction between this position and the next one, Tensions with Trusting External Authority, is that in the latter position, individuals recognize the dilemmas inherent in viewing knowledge as certain and relying on others to define their identity and relationships. Those using this meaning-making position became increasingly aware of—and concerned about—subjectivity. As they encountered conflicting expectations, they struggled to figure out what to believe, how to define themselves, and how to manage pleasing others. The primary distinction between this and the next meaning-making position, Recognizing Shortcomings of Trusting External Authority, is that in the latter position, there is an increasing acceptance of uncertainty and the emerging recognition of the need to hold one's own opinions, be oneself, and not be driven by living up to others' expectations. Here, however, the challenge to be oneself is releasing one's reliance on external sources without having an alternative approach to use instead. Thus, even at the most advanced of the external positions, reliance on external influence remains, albeit now alongside a clear recognition of its shortcomings. Developing the capacity to turn to internally evaluated sources to decide what to believe and to guide one's identity and relationships emerges in the Crossroads, the topic of the next chapter.

Entering the Crossroads: Predominantly External Positions

T HE FOCUS OF MEANING MAKING described in this chapter reflects the transition out of an external frame of reference into a new meaning-making structure, the Crossroads (see Figure 1). We describe two positions that reflect variations of predominantly externally defined meaning making in which some internal meaning making is beginning to emerge: Questioning External Authority [E(I)] and Constructing the Internal Voice (E-I). Questioning External Authority reflects a transition out of solely external meaning making and into the Crossroads. Constructing the Internal Voice reflects the external segment of the Crossroads in which both external and internal meaning-making structures are fully operating, but the internal structure functions in the service of the external one. Each position is illustrated with interview quotes to highlight its essence and the distinctions between the two.

Questioning External Authority

We define the Questioning External Authority [E(I)] position as a meaning-making position that is primarily external but also involves an emerging sign of internal voice; thus, it reflects a transition out of a solely external meaning-making structure and a way into the Crossroads. The title of this position connotes an awareness of the option or need to stop depending on external influence totally (sometimes because some external influence articulates this), but a lack of awareness about how to relate differently to external authority.

Kari B. Taylor served as coauthor of this chapter.

The person using this meaning-making position sees the possibility of another way of making meaning but is not sure how to construct it. "The *ability* to perceive the possibility of a *new* way of making meaning" (Lahey and others, 1988, p. 78) is accompanied by "the inability to do so in any way other than bent to the purposes of structure of the *old* way of making meaning" (Lahey and others, 1988, p. 78). The majority of the person's story suggests reliance on external sources for knowledge, self-definition, and social relations, despite the recognition of the possibility for an internal voice. For example, a person who uses this meaning-making structure begins to question authorities' plans, realizes the dilemma of external definition, and sees the need to craft one's own vision, develop one's internal identity, and bring one's identity to relationships (Baxter Magolda, 2001b). This awareness of the possibility for internal voice may be seen in only one dimension or across the three dimensions. A beginning awareness of how the person constructs her or his world, identity, or relationships in comparison to how external others construct them emerges as the first sign of internal voice. The external voice is clearly still in charge and although some tension exists there is not yet any substantive struggle or conflict between the two voices.

Individuals transition away from external meaning making and enter the Crossroads as they begin to differentiate between their own constructions of their identity, relationships, and beliefs and those of others. Cognitively, they recognize the possibility of making decisions based on a set of values and beliefs they have internally constructed, yet they are not yet clear on how they form beliefs. In the intrapersonal dimension, they are still in the process of discovering what they value and who they are. This complicates their ability to make internally based decisions.

Justine, a WNS participant, was home-schooled from kindergarten through her senior year in high school. She also completed thirty-two college credits at a community college during her senior year of high school. She chose to attend a college based on the financial aid package because she paid her own tuition. In her first year of college, Justine expressed a perspective that exemplifies the Questioning External Authority position:

> *I feel like a lot of people my age come to college with this set of viewpoints and it's not necessarily the viewpoints that they themselves*

own. They may ascribe to them, but it's not a viewpoint that they necessarily own. And to own a viewpoint, you must understand why and where it came from. And not only that, but you need to be able to explain it courteously to somebody else and explain why you think this way and what it is exactly that you think. I think a lot of kids my age get their ideas in different areas of life from their parents, which is not a bad thing, from their teachers, and from their peers. And none of those are bad sources, but I think that it's important to be able to articulate what it is you believe, because in articulating, in writing, in putting out what you believe, you have to think through what it is exactly. It forces you to examine your standpoint around different issues.

Providing an example of an English course in which she had to examine her standpoint on a range of issues, Justine added:

[My professor has] talked about everything from the war in Iraq to euthanasia to gay and lesbian marriages and everybody has a different viewpoint. But to have to articulate that makes you think through, "Why do I think this? Is it just because my teachers told me this in high school? Is it just because I learned this from my peers? Is it just because that's what everybody thinks, that's the most widely accepted view? Or is it because that's what I really think and I can back it up?"

Ultimately Justine recognizes a distinction between viewpoints she adopts from others and viewpoints she owns, and she is actively working to sort out which viewpoints fit into the latter category. Although she has not yet settled on a certain set of beliefs and values, she understands the importance of discovering not only what she thinks but also how or why she is forming these values and beliefs.

Interpersonally, individuals who are entering the Crossroads can identify how external sources such as their friends' and family members' views influence them, though they are not yet able to overcome or coordinate these influences.

They sometimes rely on others' validation to enact their own thinking. Justine describes this process in her relationship with her brother:

> *Once you realize that something is affecting you negatively, you have to make a conscious process, a conscious habit to break that process. Because you can't change your circumstances, but you can change your reactions. My older brother is one of my best friends and, so, a lot of times getting on the phone and talking to him and saying, "Look. This is what I'm worrying about. This is what I'm stressed out about." And he'll say, "You don't need to worry about that. Things are going to be fine. You need to focus on doing the next thing. I know who you are and I believe in you, and even though I can't help you tangibly, I know who you are and I know that you're going to make it." So, speaking with people who speak positively into your life is very important, but also being able to bring back and control your own thoughts and having that self-discipline and saying, "You know what? I'm just going to do the next thing."*

Justine is aware of when she allows worrying to increase her stress level and knows that breaking that process is necessary. However, she relies on the external validation her brother provides to enact her self-discipline and control her thoughts and behavior.

During her sophomore year, Justine shared what she did when she had a difficult decision to make: "I talk to people who matter a lot to me. And that's a huge part of what I do." Justine explained that she asked the advice of people she thought had relevant experience related to her decisions. She also considered her own instincts, saying, "I look at my potential and ask myself how—how better or more fuller will my potential be on the path that I'm going right now?" Justine revealed some sense of an internal voice by considering her own thoughts about her potential, but she said it was still "huge" to explore others' perspectives. Two years later, describing her hopes about her senior-year recital, she was still leaning on external influences:

I have always wanted to play . . . Second Hungarian Rhapsody in C-minor. But it's a gorgeous piece and it has two very different sections and they're both just extravagant and fun and interesting to listen to and they're totally different from each other, but they're huge and they're very virtuoso in nature. So, it's a very showy piece but it's just so much fun and just big, kind of just go-out-with-a-bang deal. So I kind of want to play that, but I don't know if my teacher's going to look at me like I'm nuts when I tell her that. I've also looked at Beethoven's Appassionato Sonata, the 57. It kind of starts out—and it sort of to me—sounds like the beginning of the Star Spangled Banner, but it moves into something that I just really love, a theme that I just really love. So, I'll ask her about that and see what she thinks. I'll probably do something baroque, contemporary, I'll do a couple of Moszkowski Preludes; Vladimir Horowitz does them. And he plays them so fast and I have seen him do them as encores and, of course the audience, like, erupts in applause, so I've always wanted to do a couple of Moszkowski Preludes. So, I don't know if she'll—like I said—I don't know if she'll let me do any of this. I haven't really picked out my [repertoire], but I'm hoping I get to do at least one of those pieces, . . . but we'll see; kind of go out with a bang.

Justine's passion for these various musical pieces is clear in her comments, yet she still defers to her music teacher for approval of her choices. Although she initially frames this as seeing what the teacher thinks, she indicates that the teacher may not allow her to do these pieces. Justine's internal voice appears to be gaining strength, and although the context is such that her teacher may need to sign off on the selections she will perform, she is framing the choice by how she has seen other performers use the pieces in other contexts, not using criteria for what might work well for her in this context, or allowing for legitimate concerns her teacher might raise.

Lauren, a participant in Baxter Magolda's study, grew up in a closely knit family and maintained close relationships with her parents and sister throughout college and adulthood. She articulated what occurred when important others' views differed from her instincts in this story about taking her boyfriend home to meet her parents:

> He came home with me to [my parents' house] and I was totally gung-ho. I'm like, "This is it; I know it." And then after they gave me their feedback, they liked him but they were just not sure. And after they said that, all of a sudden I didn't like him as much anymore. It was nothing that he did to me; it was not the way he acted. It was nothing. But it was because of what they said, all of a sudden I started changing my mind. Yes, that's exactly true. But then my sister, on the other hand, is the opposite and is like, "Just go with how you feel." And my friends, my close friends here are like, "Just go with how you feel." So now it's gotten better. I'm trying to really think of what I want and not what they want. So this relationship is continuing, which they're not upset about at all, but I will tell you they have told me, "Come on, this really isn't going to work. It's too far." And that does affect me. But I'm really trying to take the attitude where maybe I need to find out for myself. But I will admit always in the back of my mind what they think still lingers over my decisions [Baxter Magolda, 2001b, p. 99].

Lauren was working hard to "try to take the attitude" that she should use her internal voice. Like Lauren, those entering the Crossroads can see discrepancies between what others want for them and what they want for themselves, but they lack the confidence in and clarity about their beliefs and values necessary to act on what they want for themselves. Lauren's example, which is from her mid-twenties, highlights all three dimensions: interpersonal (in defining her relationships with her boyfriend, parents, and sister), intrapersonal (finding out what she values), and cognitive (how to make decisions based on her beliefs).

Seeing the Need for an Internal Voice

In essence, individuals who make meaning using the Questioning External Authority position continue to rely on external sources, yet they start to see the importance of developing their internal voice. They explore similarities as well as differences between how others think and act and how they want to think and act. This active exploration leads them to thoughtfully (and sometimes tentatively) question how to construct their own identity, relationships, and worldview.

Constructing the Internal Voice

In the Constructing the Internal Voice (E-I) position, both external and internal meaning-making structures are actively present and competing for dominance, but overall, the external forces still edge out the internal; for this reason, it fits within the external segment of the Crossroads. This position extends beyond the awareness of a new way of making meaning (characteristic of the Questioning External Authority position) to actively working on constructing a new way of making meaning. Yet this new internal structure is not yet dominant as the person "slips back" (Lahey and others, 1988, p. 84) toward the external structure more often than using the new internal one. The new internal structure allows for taking the external structure as object, and thus individuals experience greater tension as their internal voice competes with external voices for dominance. The internal voice is growing because the person is exploring how she or he wants to construct beliefs, identity, and relationships. The external may be predominant in some contexts, the internal in other contexts, yet the external still tends to override the internal. The person is "controlled" by the external but fighting to get the internal to take over.

Discussing her most important learning during her senior year in college, Justine offered this commentary:

> It's okay to test your values in a safe arena, and change what you think about things or come back to what you originally thought; I feel like I've done a lot of that this past year with guys and also with my relationships with guys and then also with my relationships with my girlfriends and drinking and all these different things. I feel like I've had the opportunity to try things out, but have learned that it's okay to change what I think about something and also to reevaluate

and maybe come back to what I originally thought. That's been the biggest thing I've learned this past year.

Asked to explain what she meant, she elaborated:

Making decisions that I feel like weren't the best decisions but I learned a lot from, you know, having specific boundaries for myself for so long and then—like I always knew, before I was twenty-one you can't drink, so that's not even an option. But then when you turn twenty-one, I've always thought being drunk is detrimental, but I had the opportunity to try that out and I don't think there's anything catastrophically wrong with it, you know, in a safe scenario. But learning that, "Okay, that was fun but I really have no desire to do it again." You know, and kind of coming back again to where I was before thinking that, "Yes, I'll drink, but getting drunk is just not for me." Or with guys, you know, being in a couple of short relationships and learning that the reason that I have the values and morals and standards that I do is because it keeps me a confident, happy person and that I don't need to look for self-worth in another individual, whether it's a guy or a girl or a teacher or parent. So, I think kind of testing the waters in both of those situations has enabled me to say, "You know, it's okay to reevaluate and it's okay to go back to right where you started from," or "It's okay to change what you thought your values were."

Justine's explorations led her to reconsider her values in some cases and reaffirm them in other cases. Her insight that she does not need to look for self-worth outside herself conveys that she is increasingly aware of the shortcomings of external meaning making. She does not explicitly articulate how she is going about defining her self-worth, but there are hints that she has started to look for it internally. She appears to be using her internal voice to make decisions about relationships and behavior.

Lauren articulated the tenuous balance between external and internal voices more explicitly in her continued story about her happiness versus her parents' happiness. She gained some perspective on their hesitations about her relationship when her mother shared that she was afraid Lauren would move away to where her boyfriend worked. Lauren reported that she had changed her thinking about the situation:

> *I think there are some things that have changed, i.e., the relationship with my parents; the decision of the one that needs to be happy is me—and them—but it's most important that I am; the comfort level with them and talking to them about maybe some personal things; familiarity and the comfortableness with my job. And I would say, you know, if you do well, you're going to build more self-confidence in yourself, too. . . . And you learn more about life and maybe you start realizing some things. I would think, too, and I know I'm young to be thinking about this, but I know of somebody my age who passed away this summer. And I'm one that—you know, I always think about that life isn't forever. But when people that you know—and my father always told me this—start passing away, then you really realize, "Man, you'd better be happy and life is short." So I think maybe from the past year—and I try to work at this—I try to make sure that, "You're happy and do what you want to do." I'm not a huge risk-taker, so maybe, "Take a little bit more risks in life." None that would be detrimental, but if you want to do something, you know, go do it. Because you never know. You could be in some accident tomorrow; you don't know. And I think I've just started to think about that more when I hear of people that I know dying from cancer or, you know, things as horrible as that, when you think, "I'm too young for this to happen." But I'm not. I'm really not. So maybe I'm really trying to take the attitude, you know, "If you want to do it, do it." As long as it's not going to be the end of the world, you have nothing to lose. So I've been trying to take that attitude more in life, you know, as I get older. It's also as I see my parents get older, too. That kind of—it makes me a little scared, which it shouldn't. But I definitely see them aging, and as I see them age I know that they're not going to be here forever.*

So really, "Try to make the best of the time that's there." So I would say that that's one area that I've really tried to change.

A number of dynamics converge here to push Lauren to rely on her internal voice: an increasingly open relationship with her parents, greater self-confidence, placing her happiness as slightly more important than that of her parents, and realizing that life is fragile. However, her tone is fraught with trying to take the attitude of doing what she wants to do, taking more risks, and making the best of life. She can articulate it clearly, suggesting that her internal voice is strengthening, yet she has to keep pushing herself in her own mind to act on it. It would be another eighteen months before Lauren acted on her internal voice to move to join her boyfriend and find out for herself whether it was right for her.

Developmental Progression in Entering the Crossroads

Examples of individuals' meaning making as they entered the Crossroads focused on recognizing differences among their perceptions and others' perceptions of their identity, relationships, and worldview. As a result of this recognition, they began to actively and critically question whom they wanted to be, how they wanted to relate to the world around them, and how they came to know what to believe.

The primary distinction between the Questioning External Authority position and the Constructing the Internal Voice position is that the meaning-making capacity at the latter position enables one not only to see the possibility for an internal voice, but also to start work on actively constructing this internal voice. Students in both positions of the predominantly external segment of the Crossroads began to look inward to start crafting their own beliefs and values rather than outward to others to define and shape their identity, relationships, and worldviews. Despite the emergence of the internal meaning-making structure, the external meaning-making structure still predominates. That balance shifts as individuals moved to the predominantly internal segment of the Crossroads, as we explore in the next chapter.

Leaving the Crossroads: Predominantly Internal Positions

T HIS CHAPTER DESCRIBES THE TWO POSITIONS in the second segment of the Crossroads: Listening to the Internal Voice and Cultivating the Internal Voice (see Figure 1). These two positions reflect variations of predominantly internally defined meaning making in which some external meaning making remains but is no longer dominant. We use two individuals' stories, constructed through interview quotations, to highlight the distinctions between Listening to the Internal Voice and Cultivating the Internal Voice and show two different possibilities for moving from one position to the next.

Listening to the Internal Voice

The Listening to the Internal Voice (I-E) position is the first on the developmental journey where the internal voice is more prominent than external influences. This position represents the beginning of the internal segment of the Crossroads. Here, individuals have developed the ability to simultaneously look inward and use their internal voice to make decisions, as well as recognize how they are processing and being influenced by others' points of views. Although they still occasionally internalize others' points of view, they now take responsibility for doing so. An individual who has shifted to this position from Constructing the Internal Voice works on developing his or her own distinct point of view by listening carefully to his or her internal voice and trying to hear this internal voice over the noise and clutter from the external

---

Kari B. Taylor served as coauthor of this chapter.

environment. Ultimately the internal voice has taken over, but external voices still pull on and compete with the internal voice. Overall, the internal edges out the external.

Cultivating the Internal Voice

The next position, Cultivating the Internal Voice [I(E)], represents a pathway out of the Crossroads and into a more fully developed internal meaning-making structure. At this position, the individual is now actively cultivating his or her internal voice and engaging in introspection to analyze interests, goals, and desires. The internal voice is becoming more firmly established and now mediates most external influences as the person makes decisions. Lahey and others' (1988) description of the emergence of the self-authoring mind notes a frame of reference similar to this position: "The self is now itself a generator of its own points of view. . . . Other selves are let out of the job of providing self-determining points of view and can now be related to as persons whose views and feelings can be cared for, thought about, weighed or related to, from the perspective of one's own system of meaning" (pp. 68–69). Nonetheless, the ability to distinguish one's own point of view from that of others remains tenuous. Individuals using this position have to consciously work not to slip back into their former tendency of allowing others' points of view to subsume their own point of view. The arduous steps they take to filter out others' reactions or keep their own interests firmly in focus demonstrate that the external meaning-making structure has not fully receded to the background.

Variations in Leaving the Crossroads

Our participants demonstrated considerable variation in working their way out of the Crossroads due to multiple personal and environmental contexts. Next we contrast two participants' experiences to illustrate the multiple pathways out of the Crossroads.

Diana, a WNS participant, is a first-generation college student who credits her mother for encouraging her to be an individual and not succumb to peer pressure. Diana began describing the ongoing process of accepting her sexual identity during her second year of college:

It was important for me to come out while I was in college just because I've had to hide it in secret and it was, it was eating me up, to be honest with you. In high school, I wasn't, I knew that there was something different about me and at the beginning of high school, I couldn't put a name to it. . . . I was afraid. I mean I had seen other people come out in high school and the negative reaction of people and the words and just torment they had to go through and I was like, "I can't do that. I'm too, I can't do it." It was, I was, "I'm not that brave" [laughs].

Diana's statement that hiding her true sexual identity was eating her up reflects the tension she was experiencing between her own viewpoint and others' viewpoints on being gay; this tension is a characteristic of the Crossroads. Diana's reflection on her high school experience demonstrates that she had gained the ability to articulate how and why others' viewpoints had shaped her decisions in high school. This ability to recognize the effect of external influences indicates that she was standing on the internal side of the Crossroads: Listening to the Internal Voice.

Diana went on to explain her decision to come out once she was in college:

Once I got to college I was like, "I can't deny this anymore." And so I came out and it was great. Like I felt free and now I'm ready to come out to my family, to really, you know, come out, you know, to be free of this secret I'm hiding. . . .

Two of my friends are gay and they were out. They've been out since high school and then when they come to college, the reaction that my [friends] got from people around them was supportive. No one really like made a big deal out of it . . . I think seeing them kind of in the positive light that they were in, that, how people accepted them and they were still the person, you know, besides being gay, they were still themselves. I think seeing that just kind of made me comfortable, you know, 'cause I think if [it] had been someone, that it was a negative reaction to them, I probably would have stayed in the closet.

Diana also noted:

> I was afraid [to come out] because I didn't know how people would
> take it, but the great thing about my friends [was] that they, when
> I came out to them they were like, "Oh, we knew." [laughs] You
> know, they were talking like, "We were waiting for you to,"
> you know, they kind of were really, "So you're still [Diana]." . . .
> My thing was like I'm still me. It's just one part of who I am.

As Diana entered college, the balance between her external and internal
meaning-making structures shifted, and she began to realize that she needed to
express her own sexual identity regardless of others' perceptions. Her statement
that she could no longer deny her sexual identity reflects that her internal voice
was growing strong enough to withstand challenges or criticisms she perceived
she would face from her external environment. The choice to come out, in and
of itself, is not necessarily a sign of movement toward the internal side of the
Crossroads. However, Diana grew up in a context in which societal expectations
imbued being gay with a negative connotation; thus, her decision to come out
represented a choice to listen to her internal voice despite opposing external
voices. In essence, her internal meaning-making structure had begun to edge
out her external meaning-making structure. As Diana saw her friends in college
receive support and acceptance for being gay, she gained confidence in expressing her own sexual identity and was able to lean toward using her internal voice
more fully. She continued to worry about others' perceptions, but she no longer
allowed the possibility of negative reactions to prevent her from coming out.

As Diana reflected on how coming out had affected her, her internal voice
mediated most external influences, which signified a move to Cultivating the
Internal Voice:

> I think coming out has helped me grow in that I don't hide any-
> thing. I don't feel the need to hide anymore . . . especially on cam-
> pus, it's like, "This is who I am. You accept me for me or you don't,
> you know." Where before I was like always, "Oh, well, this is only
> one part of me" or I would put on a facade about this, you know,

and pretend to be someone I wasn't. Where now, it's like I'm comfortable being myself and I think I've become so comfortable on campus being myself that now when I go home, it's like I can't go back to the person I used to be and feeling [the need] to hide, so that's why I've come to terms with having to come out to my family, so that I can be the same person I am on campus at home.

Diana added that she found the decision to come out to her family scary but necessary. She noted, "I've come to terms with it if it is a positive [or] if it's a negative. I've come to terms with that. It might not be a positive reaction, but I'm ready for it and I need just to let them know what, who I am." Her acknowledgment that coming out to her family was scary for her demonstrated that she was still working on maintaining an emotional distance from negative reactions. Yet her desire to feel comfortable being herself both on campus and at home and to integrate her sexual identity with other aspects of herself (rather than separate it as "only one part") represents interpersonal and intrapersonal growth. She was now using her internal voice more consistently, even amid challenges or resistance from her family. She had stopped holding others responsible for creating a positive perception of being gay and had begun weighing and evaluating others' perspectives.

Diana began her college experience on the internal side of the Crossroads given that she could make a distinction between her viewpoint and others' viewpoints, as well as recognize the role she played in allowing others to influence her. She was able to make a relatively quick transition from Listening to the Internal Voice to Cultivating the Internal Voice because she found support in college for using her internal voice. During her fourth year, she explained that she began to embrace different aspects of her identity once she had started to interact with people "who were really free thinkers and really accepted who they were." She elaborated, "I feel like that kind of rubbed off on me . . . and I think that it started to help me like, really, you know, love who I am no matter like the flaws that I have." Once she gained support for using her internal voice to make meaning of her identity, beliefs, and values, she increasingly gained confidence in expressing who she was and how she saw the world. She took another step toward developing a fully internal meaning-making structure as she decided to come out to her family and be her true self in multiple contexts. Because she continued to worry about losing herself (at least to a degree) when faced with strong viewpoints that conflicted with her own, she still used a trace of external meaning making.

While Diana had to sort through and weed out clutter from her high school environment, Phillip, a participant in Baxter Magolda's study, had to filter out noise from his family context. He reported that he "loved his parents to death" and valued their advice. Ideally Phillip wanted to pursue a career in music, but he struggled to follow his dream given his competing interest to please his parents. Describing how his family's way of operating influenced his ability to pursue a career he found truly meaningful, he stated:

> *The family is very conservative. We don't do anything until we think about it for five years. Nothing is ever decided on a whim. It's like, "Let's see, I want to buy a car, oh, geez, next year. So I better start thinking about it right now," stuff like that. It can be really difficult to take risks in that kind of situation. It really can. And it takes a lot of determination to say, "Well, this is what I believe in and I'm going to continue with it come hell or high water." There were times when I said, "Well, they're right." I gave in and I said, "They're right. I should just forget about this." But I'm thinking, "Well, why are you going to do that? You don't know what might happen to you tomorrow. Suppose something comes along?" [Baxter Magolda, 2001b, p. 105].*

He further explained his struggle to listen to his own voice amid those of his parents:

> *But when it comes from your parents, there is a big impact. I don't know. I guess it's just the background that I have, but I wasn't very much of a rebellious child. So whatever the folks said was pretty much like, "Well, you've got to pay attention to that." I love them both to death, but the thing is that their interests are different from mine. They changed probably once I became an adult because, like I say, they probably had their ideas. My dad probably wanted me to go*

into sales a long time ago. And I knew that wasn't for me. But once you're 20, 21, and you're out of school, it's like you just want to— you want so bad to take charge of your life and you want to have it turn out right. It really helps you to achieve that goal when you've got support. And especially, like I say, from your parents, from your good friends. But when they're telling you, "Oh, no, you don't want to do this. Why did you do that?" you fall into this role like, "Oh, well, bad boy. Slap your hands." I did for a while, too. Moving back home was not a—I think I regressed actually. I fell back into the role of the dutiful son and that is just not, it's not a positive outlook on life. It doesn't give you anything. It's just like, "Well, you're doing something for somebody else and not for yourself." . . . I am the proverbial rolling stone right now, the free wind, or whatever you want to call it. I'm able to make my own decisions; I can take peo- ple's advice, but it gives you a sense of accomplishment, right or wrong, if you've made the decision, you know, and you have to live with it [Baxter Magolda, 2001b, pp. 104–105].

After he graduated from college, Phillip's meaning making varied, but it con- sistently reflected the tensions between external and internal that are charac- teristic of the Crossroads. He had gained the ability to distinguish between his interests and those of his parents. For example, he realized that a career in sales—the professional path his father wanted him to pursue—was not for him. Yet he did not keep his own interests in focus. His statement that he "fell back into the role of the dutiful son" when he moved back home indicates that external influences overpowered his internal voice at times and that he regressed to Constructing the Internal Voice. Thus, he did not consistently stay at Listening to the Internal Voice; moreover, unlike Diana, he did not quickly move through the Crossroads. Rather, he vacillated between these two positions. Because he had deeply internalized his parents' hesitancy toward taking risks and because he had always followed his parents' expectations, he experienced significant tension when he faced the decision to move away from home and pursue his own goals. His ability to recognize how his family back- ground influenced his decisions and his desire to do something for himself (rather than for someone else) demonstrates that he had the capacity to use his internal meaning-making structure to edge out his external meaning-making structure. Yet he sometimes fell back when the pull of external voices became particularly strong.

As Phillip contemplated how to take charge of his life, he eventually found support for acting on his own goals. He explained:

> It was just, "Oh, the future is bleak and this and that." It was just a matter of me telling myself, "Okay, this is what I want. And what do I need to do to get it?" I can listen to other people's advice and take it with a grain of salt. I can do that until I'm blue in the face. Is that going to get me where I want to go? No. It takes action, not words. And the attitude of people in my hometown was just absolutely bleak. The main industry in there just plummeted really badly. So everybody's got this cloud of doom over their head, including my parents. . . . So I was just really in the doldrums. But I decided to just pull myself out of that and it took a lot of strength within to say, "Look, you've just got to get out of this situation." In fact, you know, going back down to Miami [University] during November to visit some friends kind of convinced me because I talked to some of the faculty. They were really supportive. I told them that I was planning on leaving the Midwest and going out East. And they said, "Well, do it. What's holding you back? If you can do it, do it by all means because you just don't know what could happen to you. Things could be bad, but again, just think, something could happen after you're there a couple of months that could change your outlook, could be real promising for you in the future." So I kind of weighed the evidence and decided to come out [to the East Coast]. And it's been for the good. I think the whole experience has changed my outlook. I'm not going to ever get myself into a rut where I'm saying, "Oh, well, whatever I've done in the past is just worthless. I've got to pay more attention to other people's advice." Because if you do that, everybody's got their own opinion on something. If you continue to listen to everything that everybody says, you're going to be a

chameleon; you're going to be changing from year to year, doing this, doing that [Baxter Magolda, 2001b, pp. 103–104].

The faculty members to whom Phillip spoke helped him lean toward the internal side of the Crossroads, Listening to the Internal Voice. In essence, they served as a counterbalance to his parents, and the faculty's advice gave Phillip confidence in using his internal voice. In addition, Phillip had reached the conclusion that he had to make a change and get out of his current situation; thus, he was ready to start using his internal voice. Because Phillip then evaluated the advice he received from various individuals and made a final decision that aligned with his interests, he demonstrated the capacity to hear his internal voice amid noise from the external environment. Once he left his parents' home and moved to the East Coast, he continued to listen to his internal voice. He explained:

> *I realized there were so many opportunities that I could take advantage of, the fact that I didn't have any debt, the fact that I had parents, whether negative or not, [who] were willing to go along with me after I just consistently knocked them over the head with it and said, "This is what I want to do." I was able to get where I wanted to go.*

Phillip's internal voice, similar to Diana's, grew more prominent as he expressed his goals and interests even in the midst of his parents' hesitations. He was able to explain what he wanted to do despite the possibility that his parents did not wholly agree with his decision. Ultimately he shifted his meaning making to Cultivating the Internal Voice as he kept his goals and interests in the foreground even when his parents expressed other perspectives.

He continued to cultivate his internal voice by seeking out additional support for pursuing his own goals. He noted:

> *For me if I am surrounded by a bunch of positive people, I feel I can do things. In 1995 I went on vacation to see Aunt Arlene—a positive person in our family. She has turmoil, but comes out on top. She has a positive mental attitude. She was in ill health, but still spry. I told her about my dilemmas. She asked me why I didn't*

do what I wanted. She said there is a way. She told me not to give
up hope. Taking that, I think I have learned to apply that in other
areas of my life. Instead of being reactionary, I'm finding ways to
get what I want without making bunches of waves that will be to
my detriment [Baxter Magolda, 2001b, p. 106].

Phillip's statement that he had moved from "being reactionary" to being proactive about getting what he wants reflects his transition to Cultivating the Internal Voice. Although he still looked for external support from Aunt Arlene to strengthen his internal voice, a sign that he still felt some pull from external influences, he was now able to use his own point of view to guide his decisions in multiple areas of his life. He was also learning to use his internal voice to manage others' reactions to avoid creating distractions that might be detrimental to his goals.

Phillip's pathway through the Crossroads was less direct than Diana's. The tension he experienced between his own point of view and that of others persisted for several years as he struggled to extract himself from his family context and reframe his relationship with his parents. Yet once he found sufficient support for using his internal voice, he, too, was able to keep his internal voice in the foreground and allow external voices to recede to the background.

Developmental Progression in Leaving the Crossroads

A key characteristic across the four Crossroads positions is the increasing trust individuals have using their internal voice. Although the internal voice was dominant in meaning making at the Listening to the Internal Voice position, external voices remained present and created tension when they did not align with the internal voice. As individuals prepared to leave the Crossroads having Cultivated the Internal Voice, they grew better able to manage external influences. Ultimately they gained the capacity to decide which external influences to pay attention to and how to let such influences affect them. Thus, these individuals were better able to weigh and critique external influences, and these influences subsequently lost their pull as primary driving forces in their lives.

Self-Authorship: Internal Positions

THIS CHAPTER DESCRIBES THE THREE POSITIONS within the Internal, or Self-Authoring, meaning-making structure on the journey to self-authoring one's life (see Figure 1). These three, designated as Trusting the Internal Voice (Ia), Building an Internal Foundation (Ib), and Securing Internal Commitments (Ic), reflect variations of internally defined, or self-authored, meaning making. In all three, the internal voice is the mainstay; the overall structure for knowledge, identity, and social relations is internally grounded. The internal voice mediates external influence, critically analyzing it and making judgments about it based on internal criteria.

Three positions within this self-authoring structure are evident in Baxter Magolda's (2008, 2009a) study. The initial position is Trusting the Internal Voice. Increasing use of the internal voice engenders confidence in it and decreases the likelihood of being pulled back to the former tendency to subsume one's views to others' views. Trusting the Internal Voice leads to taking responsibility for constructing knowledge, identity, and relationships and using the internal voice as the mechanism through which to analyze and coordinate external influence. Once a person trusts the internal voice, she or he is able to Build an Internal Foundation by integrating beliefs, identity, and social relations into internally held commitments. The internal foundation becomes a filter through which to process external circumstances and a guide for shaping one's reactions to them. As the foundation becomes more comprehensive, the person transitions to Securing Internal Commitments by living out these

---

Rosemary J. Perez served as coauthor of this chapter.

conceptualizations. Here, the internal foundation becomes second nature, such that some external influences go unnoticed and those that are important enough to attract attention are processed more readily through the internal foundation. Because only a small group of WNS participants demonstrated signs of internal meaning making by their senior year in college, we draw on a participant from Baxter Magolda's longitudinal study to illustrate these positions. Each position is illustrated with interview quotations to highlight its essence and the distinctions among the three.

Trusting the Internal Voice

Sufficient cultivation of the internal voice led to trusting it to coordinate external influence. Baxter Magolda's (2008) participants recognized that external events were beyond their control, but their reactions to external events were within their control. As young adults worked to use their internal voices to shape their reactions to external events, they determined "when to make something happen versus when to let something happen" (p. 279). Trust evolved over time as they gained confidence in their internal voices in each developmental dimension and in multiple contexts.

In the cognitive dimension, increased trust in the internal voice allowed young adults to take ownership of how they made meaning of the world rather than looking to others to construct their perspective. While they were aware of others' opinions and perspectives, they tended to be introspective and engage in reflection as a means of making sense of external events. Intrapersonally, individuals recognized that they were in control of their emotions and were able to create their own happiness. Acknowledging the malleability of emotions was particularly important as young adults navigated challenging situations and determined their responses to external events. Within the interpersonal dimension, growing trust in the internal voice led them to continuously reevaluate relationships, particularly ones that were not grounded in a sense of mutuality and respect. Some lamented the loss of relationships that did not provide space for their own internal voice, while others pondered how to construct new interdependent relationships.

Evan, a participant in Baxter Magolda's longitudinal study, lacked career focus early in college. After realizing that he was distracted by involvement in his fraternity, he transferred to another college and majored in communications. He landed a job in commercial real estate during his senior year and continued in that position after graduation. A key component of Evan's approach to life was striving to improve himself and his performance in whatever he did. This trait, in combination with his organizational skills, netted him considerable autonomy in his work role. This autonomy and his interest in improving his performance led him to a new awareness of how he worked and how he related to the world around him. He explained:

> *The most dramatic difference between before and after was my ability to think, and the subsequent confidence in my abilities and trust in my decisions. I have developed my own approach to solving problems, one that has proven to me to be a good one, and one that has proven to be a good teacher. When it becomes apparent to me that I have relied on this ability, I often try to remember what I did before I began to understand how my mind worked [Baxter Magolda, 2001b, pp. 121–122].*

Understanding how his mind worked helped him devise problem-solving approaches that were successful for him, which in turn increased his trust in himself and simultaneously decreased his reliance on others for support or guidance in his work. Growth in the cognitive arena yielded growth in the intrapersonal dimension, as evident in this comment:

> *As my personality and sense of self have really begun to develop and become more refined, my ability to direct my life accordingly has become increasingly confident. As I realize who I am, and what is important to me, it becomes easier for me to establish my priorities. Identifying and arranging my priorities has helped me to develop a "road map" for reaching short- and long-term goals. Don't get me wrong, I am not trying to predict the future and I by no means know exactly what I want, but I have developed a general idea and use my knowledge as a guide [Baxter Magolda, 2001b, p. 122].*

Increasing confidence in his abilities to think and in his identity led to subsequent changes in his approach to relationships as well:

I find that I am constantly rebalancing my identity in relationship to others. With my parents' divorce two years ago, and the purchase of my home, I am becoming a central figure in the extended family and have left behind my "youth" oriented identity. At work, my identity continues to grow almost as fast as my personal identity. Since I began with the current crew 2 1/2 years ago, I have been titled Asset Manager, Senior Asset Manager, Assistant Vice President, and now Vice President. My identity within the group has changed very much. I owe this to my abilities in being aware of how my mind works and dealing with my personal set of realities [Baxter Magolda, 2001b, pp. 122–123].

Changes in Evan's family life and his work setting led him to the conclusion that his realities were beyond his control. Yet his success in problem solving and adjusting to new roles convinced him that he could control his reactions to these events. As he improved his work performance, he refined his ways of learning and thinking through situations, using the new knowledge to guide his future action. As he worked through family changes, he reflected internally on his identity and applied the insights he gained to establish his priorities. Numerous external forces were at play here as Evan learned to deal with what he called his "personal set of realities." Trusting his internal voice enabled him to analyze those external forces and choose how to react to them based on his internally established priorities. Trusting his problem-solving ability, his sense of identity, and his adult relationships set the stage for Evan to begin building an internal foundation.

Building an Internal Foundation

Trusting their internal voices enabled individuals to mediate external influences as they internally refined their beliefs, values, identities, and relationships. As a result, they took up the task of integrating their beliefs, values, identities, and relationships into a framework, or an internal foundation, to guide how they reacted to external influences. Some referred to this as a philosophy of life. They used their internal foundations to make decisions, realign aspects of their lives with their internal beliefs, and focus on what was most important to them in times of crisis. Acting on these internal foundations as they were constructing them yielded feedback that sometimes led to working further on trusting their internal voices. For example, using the internal foundation sometimes illuminated fragile areas of internal beliefs, identities, or relationships that were in tension with external forces, but they had not yet figured out how to manage these tensions. Reflecting on those and processing how to manage those external influences meant working to solidify the internal voice in those areas. These two positions worked in conjunction with each other because trusting the internal voice was essential to building an internal foundation that in turn strengthened the internal voice.

Trusting his internal voice enabled Evan to construct a philosophy of life. One component of his philosophy involved shifting work to constitute only one part of his identity. He took work seriously, but he kept it in perspective based on his priorities:

> *I'm very serious about work. I give anything my best effort I can whether I enjoy it or not. Once I get to my office, I take it seriously. Not so seriously where it stresses me. No point in that. When I was younger I let it get to me. When I was inexperienced. No matter what, the sun always comes up the next day. Very rarely is my work a life or death situation. There was a time when I was depressed. I took a lot from that; use that as a guidepost. It was good to get it out of the way early! Now, let's get on with things [Baxter Magolda, 2009a, p. 195].*

Performing effectively at work and managing stress effectively emerged as mainstays of Evan's evolving internal foundation. Keeping things in perspective in light of unanticipated challenges was also a mainstay of his personal life, where he was also taking on additional responsibility:

> *I have accepted a role in my extended family, not the leader, but it seems to be getting to that. I'm not ready to start my own family with kids. That is not something that I want; not now, don't know if I ever want it. When the time comes, it will be like everything*

else. If the time comes, fine. I got married early enough; I learned not to rush into things. Not everybody in my family has a house, so people have functions here. That's thrown me. I am the oldest. My family split apart; my parents divorced. Dad isn't around. I've stepped up in that area. My grandmother passed away in December; my grandfather is still around but they are no longer the "king and queen." With my grandmother gone, we've had to step up taking care of my grandfather. The rules are up for grabs. My brother is not around. I'm the hub of communication for things. I don't mind it [Baxter Magolda, 2009a, p. 196].

Evan processed these changes and made sense of them in order to avoid a recurrence of his earlier depression. As he refined his internal foundation, he developed a new outlook on life that reflected his way of reacting to his circumstances:

Now [I] just kind of accept these things; nothing ever stays the same. If you expect it, it is easier. A lot of things I am incredibly inflexible about. As far as other people and other things, I don't try to control. I've gradually gotten that way. The only way is to experience this and to see what happens when you don't take that route. The experience you accumulate can be painful but necessary. It adds to your repertoire of being able to deal with things in the future; been through it, lived, know what is coming next. It is less frightening, less mysterious [Baxter Magolda, 2001b, pp. 156–157].

In relinquishing his efforts to control other people and things, Evan focused on controlling his reactions to them, using his internal priorities and refined sense of identity and relationships as a guide. This internal foundation helped him cope with many challenges that would come his way, including his wife's pregnancy before he was sure he was ready for children, his father's incarceration, his brother's heart attack, and the World Trade Center bombing down the street from his office. Explaining how he coped with his wife's pregnancy, he said:

It was something that really frightened me for a long time—I don't know why. It is such a serious thing—being responsible for somebody

forever. It was different than getting married, if that was not right,
you could get out of it if push came to shove. Only a semi-permanent
thing, realistically. Once this went into effect, you can't undo it.
Once a child is born, you are attached to another person through
the child. Permanence, responsibility, always played a part in my
willingness to go through with it. I knew if my wife didn't just force
me, I would never do it. I needed that shove [Baxter Magolda,
2001b, pp. 157–158].

Evan's internal foundation helped him open himself up to this new responsibility despite his trepidation. It also helped him manage stress and work through conflict. Learning how to reduce his stress about external forces beyond his control, possible in large part due to his internal foundation, was a major accomplishment for Evan during his twenties.

Securing Internal Commitments

The key feature of the Securing Internal Commitments position is that it signals a shift from forming and admiring internal commitments to living them. Baxter Magolda's participants noted that they believed they were embodying these commitments as they constructed their internal foundations, but realized later that to live them meant that they became central to one's core sense of self. They described this process as one where commitments become second nature, much like breathing, and often expressed that they felt there was no other choice but to live out these commitments once they were firmly established. Securing internal commitments entailed blurring knowledge and sense of self to develop wisdom, which participants described as the ability to "know" internally and intuitively because knowledge had become central to the core self. Wisdom was also second nature as a result of living out commitments, enabling participants to integrate their internal foundations and their particular external circumstances. This yielded an increased sense of security and greater sense of freedom that came from trusting one's ability to manage what was within one's control. It also yielded an increased openness to further growth, which sometimes led participants to return to building additional trust in their voices and refining their internal foundations.

Because of his extensive workplace experience, Evan often handled the toughest problems in his commercial real estate management company. He routinely dealt with evictions and bankruptcy cases and reported that he was comfortable working through the complexities they posed:

> *Because I've repeated the same processes over and over for the past twelve years, there's a lot of skills or knowledge that I've acquired that are second nature at this point. When I do have to take on a task that I might not have taken on before, or one that's more difficult, I can process it much quicker than I used to. My blood pressure doesn't rise up above normal. Not a lot of things frighten me anymore, and I'm very patient when it comes to taking on something new. There's nothing hidden behind the curtain that I don't understand. I know the pieces of the puzzle are there, and I have the skills necessary to deal with them. So, it's not as hard as it once was [Baxter Magolda, 2009a, p. 199].*

Although Evan noted that it was experience that helped him perform tasks, the fact that his knowledge of work and himself had become second nature (reflective of securing internal commitments) helped him function comfortably in what others might view as stressful situations. He inherently knows what to do, how to approach things, and how not to be frightened by new tasks. Similarly, he was no longer frightened of being a parent because he had worked through how to approach parenting to support his daughter in becoming a strong, mature person. He had figured out how to function effectively in a mutual partnership in his marriage. Having played hockey since childhood, Evan took up refereeing professional hockey in his thirties. He quickly became successful as a referee because he was comfortable and effective in managing conflict. His internal commitments to excellent performance, constant personal improvement, maintaining a positive outlook, remaining calm, and treating others with respect permeated all of these aspects of his life. He reported that his internal commitments served him well when the World Trade Center bombing took place down the street from his office:

I was building a philosophy before 9/11, but that kind of solidified my thinking on a lot of different things, and a lot of things become less important after that. I don't quite take so much as seriously, and, on the other hand, I don't take a lot for granted anymore either. I appreciate a lot more things now, not that I didn't before, but I place a higher value on certain things as opposed to others. I had discovered that path before this, so it wasn't that much of a radical change, but uh (long pause) it did, for a few weeks, it did really shake me up [Baxter Magolda, 2009a, p. 203].

Given Evan's internal commitments, it took quite a bit to shake him up. He attributed much of his ability to keep perspective to his experience in refereeing hockey. He explained:

Refereeing . . . there are a lot of good byproducts to that for work and a lot of other situations. You just learn to deal with it and you learn patience. You learn dealing with people. You learn how to make decisions quickly; you learn how to treat people. You have to hold yourself to a higher standard than everyone else because you're in charge. I definitely think it's helped me at work. Whether it's something like holding my tongue if somebody says something or just dealing with a higher pressure situation, I definitely have developed those types of skills as a byproduct. At the level that I work at, the games are tremendously difficult most of the time. I have to focus on a second-by-second basis a lot of times because there are a lot of things going on and there's a lot that I'm responsible for. I just try to do my best, stay focused, be fair and hopefully I'm in position, make all my calls and nothing controversial happens, and I'm happy. I think I've done my job well if no one knows I was there or no one knows my name [Baxter Magolda, 2009a, p. 213].

Evan refereed professional hockey where the stakes are high and emotions run strong. It is clear from his description that his ego is not important; he is happiest if no one was aware that he was on the ice. High-pressure situations are

Evan's forte. His ease in such situations reflects his secure internal commitments: he trusts his internal voice, he is confident in his knowledge and skills, he has integrated his knowledge and identity into how he relates to others, and he manages external forces by keeping his priorities in perspective. These capacities enable him to live his commitments to excellent performance, constant improvement, calmly managing conflict and crises, and having a positive effect on those around him.

Evan's internal commitments were also clear in his relationships. In a recent interview, he described how he approached helping his twelve-year-old daughter, Kerry, handle difficult situations:

> *I practice not getting stressed. Because of scuba diving, refereeing, I'm in the situation to be stressed all the time. I put myself in these situations that most people are not capable of handling at all. I am comfortable in them. It takes a lot of practice to get like that— takes a lot of control. It does not come naturally. I try to teach younger referees and Kerry. She scuba dives with me a lot—she's a kid, and I expect her to panic at first sight of anything. I'm trying to teach her that is not how to react. We switched seats at a hockey game and she left her jacket in our other seats. I sent her back; she returned saying it was gone. I walk back and take her to the seat and it is sitting there. She went to the wrong row and went into a panic. I teach her stop, take a breath, figure out what is wrong; if you are doing something correctly, are you looking in the right place. Use that as a teaching tool to mold her. We had the same incident scuba diving. I turn my head for a second and Kerry is gone! I'm like "where in the hell did she go?" I hear her, and look up, and she has surfaced, which you are not supposed to do. So now I've got to go up and get her. We are in the middle of the Atlantic on the surface arguing—I'm like "what is the first thing I always tell you? Settle down. Get yourself together and let's go." I try to use the situation to not be an awful parent—"okay what happened? Why? What could you have done about it? Are you going to let it happen again?" She adjusts, rolls with it. It is a better way to do*

things—my parents didn't do that with me! I'm trying to break the cycle there.

Evan's security in himself and his abilities helped him not panic when his daughter temporarily disappeared during the dive. In the heat of the moment, he realized the importance of calming down to focus on teaching her how to react rather than becoming angry. His practice at not getting worked up over the years had become second nature to him.

In the same interview, Evan shared that he was no longer in contact with his father. Evan's dad lived with Evan and his family briefly, and during that time, Evan made many attempts to involve him in his hockey activities and Kerry's activities. His father declined to participate and hesitated to find meaningful employment after his incarceration. Evan tried to work out reasonable arrangements for how they could all function in the same household with the regimented organization required by Evan's work and hockey schedule. His father did not respect those requests, and finally Evan suggested that he find another place to live. His father left unexpectedly one day while Evan was at work. Evan had a difficult time with his father's attitude toward life, which he regarded as negative and reflected not taking responsibility for his circumstances. Asked how he felt about this situation, Evan shared:

> *I'm not getting dragged into that. There is plenty of other positive stuff to do and people that aren't like that. Why should the squeaky wheel get the grease in this case? There is limited time here to do what you want or accomplish what you want—nothing is static—you have to focus on good stuff. Of course bad stuff is gonna happen, but just move on.*

Because his efforts to sustain a mutual relationship were not working, Evan accepted his father as he is and shifted his focus to more positive relationships in his life. His secure internal commitments enabled him to accept this situation as a circumstance over which he had no control, and he shaped his reaction to it through his internal commitments.

Developmental Progression in Internal Meaning Making

The unfolding of these three developmental positions reflects the consolidation of internal meaning-making capacities and the evolution of a self-authored meaning-making structure. Trusting the Internal Voice focuses primarily on refining the internal voice in each of the developmental dimensions. Building an Internal Foundation shifts to crafting one's beliefs, values, identity, and relationship to the world into a philosophy of living to guide one's decisions and actions. Securing Internal Commitments reflects the solidification of this philosophy, or internal foundation, to the point that it becomes second nature and the core of one's being. As such, these internal commitments are lived out on a daily basis.

Evan's story and those of his peers in Baxter Magolda's longitudinal study reveal that while trusting the internal voice may start in early adulthood depending on personal characteristics and contextual circumstances, it took time for the internal voice to develop sufficiently to build an internal foundation. Internally constructing one's beliefs, values, identity, and relationships required significant reflection, working through tensions with external influences and realigning relationships to bring the internal voice to the forefront. This work was rarely linear, but rather evolved through reworking the internal voice as participants encountered various experiences. Participants trying out their internal voices in turn shaped their experiences. As they gained experience constructing the world with their internal voices, they refined them sufficiently to integrate into an internal foundation, another process that took time and sustained energy. Similarly, it took time and experience for the internal foundation to become second nature. Many participants reported believing they were living their commitments, only to learn that in some circumstances, they were not. This continuous refining of the self-authoring meaning-making structure emerged from facing life's challenges and finding supportive environments that helped participants learn to navigate these challenges. For most participants in Baxter Magolda's study, these self-authoring positions developed in participants' late twenties and thirties. Although we saw hints of these three positions in the WNS interview data, very few college seniors in the WNS fully demonstrated these positions, suggesting that the majority of participants' college and life experiences had not yet promoted this way of making meaning.

The portrait of these three self-authoring positions that emerged from studying adults in their twenties and thirties contributes to our ability to describe and assess the complex phenomenon of self-authored meaning making. These position descriptions help distinguish between the emergence of one's internal voice and the refinement and solidification of the internal voice.

Using the Self-Authorship Assessment Guide

THIS CHAPTER INTRODUCES our Self-Authorship Assessment Guide, which is designed to assist researchers in assessing self-evolution and the journey to self-authorship in both research and assessment contexts. These detailed instructions, along with the training information provided in the third chapter, "Development of the Ten Positions in the Journey Toward Self-Authorship," will help individual researchers or research teams as they implement this assessment process; in light of this instructional purpose, we shift our language here to speak directly to assessors.

To acknowledge the background and theoretical roots of this Guide, we first offer a brief history of its evolution. As its authors, our backgrounds and professional experiences inform its focus. We both have extensive experience assessing college student development, most notably the assessment of the models of cognitive development we have each developed; these are Baxter Magolda's (1992) Epistemological Reflection Model and King and Kitchener's (1994) Reflective Judgment Model. Both models describe the evolution of meaning making (in particular, ways of knowing in the cognitive domain), both are grounded in the constructive-developmental tradition, both were derived from longitudinal interview data, and both provide extensive information about the assessment process. Our experiences with these lines of research informed this Guide in ways we are aware of (for example, the value of listening to individuals explain their experiences) and likely in ways of which we are not yet aware.

In addition, we both serve as co-principal investigators of the Wabash National Study of Liberal Arts Education (WNS), with responsibilities for designing, implementing, and overseeing data collection and analysis of the qualitative portion of this study. In this role, we selected and trained the interviewers and summarizers and have worked on several dissertations and other studies using WNS data. Although the design of the WNS interview was deeply informed by Baxter Magolda's ongoing longitudinal study, it was adapted to the specific purposes of the WNS. Similarly, the self-authorship assessment was informed by prior work on self-authorship assessment, most notably that of Kegan and his colleagues (Lahey and others, 1988) and Baxter Magolda (see Baxter Magolda, 2001b, for a detailed description of her approach). Although our resulting Guide was based on these main resources, it was refined throughout the four-year study to reflect the insights, cautions, and lessons learned from using this process to analyze over nine hundred WNS interviews. In this and many other ways, the creation of this Guide required a team effort. In the appendix at the end of this monograph, we identify the WNS qualitative research team.

Long, detailed interviews are rich and fascinating portraits of individuals' lives. They have the potential to provide key insights into college students' educational experiences, as well as what educators can do to improve their experiences toward desired ends, such as the achievement of learning outcomes and becoming self-authoring. Rich as whole transcripts are, data reduction steps are necessary for data analysis. This is the function of the transcript summaries described here: to retain the substance of the interview while reducing the volume of data for analysis. We offer this process, based on our experience in the WNS, as an analysis process that can be adapted for use in multiple contexts.

Assessing Student Characteristics and Experience

Meaning making occurs in a context and draws on the individual's background characteristics and prior experiences. Whether your project is driven by an interest in specific collegiate learning outcomes (such as the liberal arts outcomes used in the WNS), engagement in specific types of experiences (for example, exposure to high-impact practices), or a focus on the experiences of a selected student subgroup (for example, first-generation students) or a selected campus context (for example, an organization that stresses leadership skills), gathering information about individuals' background characteristics is crucial to understanding meaning making. Thus, the background information from Phase 1, combined with the experiences that provided the impetus and contexts for meaning making, are all essential elements to understanding the development of the capacity to self-author one's life. (Figure 2 portrays these elements visually, showing how they guided both the initial structure of the WNS Interview and its iterative use over time.)

We created two complementary summaries for use in the WNS. The purposes of the first (Phase 1) summary included some that were specific to the WNS research questions. Although those purposes are narrower than that of this monograph, we introduce them here so readers can understand where and how we summarized student background characteristics and student experiences.

The broad purposes of the first section of this Guide are to provide relevant background information about the students, details about the nature of their experiences, and an initial analysis of the effects of each important experience the student shared. More specifically, the summarizer's objectives in writing this section are to:

- identify important student characteristics and any other relevant information to better understand the interview;
- identify all experiences the student selected as important and describe each experience, noting its effect on the student; the relationship of the effect to liberal arts outcomes; and whether (and, if so, how) the experience affected the student; and
- note those experiences in which the institution played an explicit role, for example, where students referenced specific institutional programs or practices.

In the context of the WNS, we referred to this as the Phase 1 summary. We offer excerpts of a Phase 1 summary to illustrate this process.

Example of a Phase 1 Summary (Excerpts)

Summary, Phase 1: [Interview ID, Interviewer Name, Summarizer Name, Date Summary was Completed]

I. Student Characteristics and Background Information

This student is a second-year woman from a wealthy family who grew up 10 minutes away from the college she attends (a private liberal arts college in southern California). As of the time of the interview, her parents were in the process of separating. She reiterated her decision from her year 1 interview to major in Child Development with minors in Spanish and Education. Her mother, grand-mother, and great-grandmother were all teachers and she plans to be a teacher as well. She has never entertained any other profession besides her parents' (an elementary school teacher and a bank president); she acknowledges that her mother is responsible for leading her to her "little dream" of becoming a teacher. She is very close with her father and has decided to move back home at the end of the current semester to be closer to him and her younger sisters. [3] (Numbers in brackets refer to the location of information or quoted materials in the tran-script and are used to show the basis for a summarizer's description.)

II. Experiences the Interviewee Identifies as Important
1. Visiting Pennsylvania (description omitted from excerpt).
2. Living in [college town] (description omitted from excerpt).
3. Social Encounter in Course Entitled, "Why Read?" [7][9–12]

Nature/quality of experience: The student was surprised when she walked into one of her classes and met someone who seemed totally different from her:

> "I remember my first day of one my classes last year, walking in and seeing a girl dressed in all black and like her hair was like bright pink and she had black makeup on and I remember her coming off as like the most random ideas for the lecture that day. And just think-ing, 'Who are you? Like what planet did you come from?'" [9]

Effect of the experience: Despite her initial shock, the student ended up appre-ciating this foreign-seeming classmate, as she recalled:

> "And I've been getting to know her, though, through group projects and stuff. It was a good experience because just talking to her and hearing her side of things, like she's really right a lot of the time, like

(Continued)

she had some great quotes from random books that I haven't even heard of to add to the discussion. And I think it's pretty cool." [9]

Even though both women are from California, the interviewee found the other student's culture to be alien in some ways:

"She's just real different like culture, like different, she had, didn't practice any religion. She was just completely removed from everything." [10]

According to the interviewee, the girl in black was admirably well read, as she describes:

"I was impressed a lot with the fact that she could draw on other works of literature or other experiences that she'd had through reading these books. And I felt that if I could do that as well, I'd be a stronger student." [10]

As part of their growing friendship, the girl in black gave the interviewee a reading list:

"I don't remember specific titles anymore, but some of it was just going as far as reading certain pieces of Shakespeare or going back and reading like *Oedipus* or something like that. And being able to relate those things to modern day stories and such, and just drawing off of things like that. I never would have thought that I would have sat down and read anything by Freud, never. And she gave me the book as a gift for the end of last year. I sat down and I read it this summer, and I'm able to draw from it, and pull in conversations, even like today in class." [10]

The student described how excited she was to see the connections between her extracurricular reading and her classes:

"And what was great about that [reading Freud] actually was that it related to my child development classes, different ideas that he had really related to child development, like the study of thought processes and the way that their relationships are with their peers and it relates now to the study with Dr. [faculty advisor] that I'm working on." [12]

(Continued)

II. Experiences the Interviewee Identifies as Important (*Continued*)

The interviewee had never been exposed to those kinds of books before, but she recognizes the benefits of reading them:

> "I'm an avid reader to begin with, but I'd never thought of reading a different genre of books. It helped me a lot. And it's helping me a lot even with my classes now." [10]

In a sense, the student rediscovered how exciting reading can be for its own sake, as she stated,

> "It was kind of just going and playing in the library, I guess. I do charity work every summer, so I work there and I read with children. And I think just going, playing in like the different aisles and like, 'Hmm, what's this one about?' And if I didn't get anything out of it that I can use in a class, I still read it; it's still a form of literature that one author is writing, like Why Read?, you know." [12]

Finally, the girl in black encouraged the student to attend some of the talks by visiting authors. The student admitted,

> "And I think that I probably wouldn't have gone to any of those if she hadn't been, 'Oh hey, I read his book. Go and read it.'" [11]

How effect relates to Liberal Arts outcomes: This experience touches upon the outcomes of Integration of Learning, Inclination to Inquire and Lifelong Learning, and Intercultural Effectiveness.

(1) *Integration of Learning:* The student has found opportunities to apply what she learned through her friend's recommended reading list to her current classes. [9][10][12]

(2) *Inclination to Inquire and Lifelong Learning:* Although the student describes herself as an avid reader, her eyes were truly opened by her exposure to a range of literary genres. [10] Furthermore, as a result of her friendship and broader literary background, as well as her growing appreciation for literature, the student is now interested in taking advantage of cultural opportunities on campus. [11][12]

(3) *Intercultural Effectiveness:* Related to the student's previous observation that she has some judgmental tendencies [7], her encounter with "the girl in black" encouraged the student to build a relationship with someone she had initially not appreciated. The student learned that seemingly "foreign" cultures can exist even within her home state. [9]

Assessing Developmental Meaning Making

The primary purpose of the second section of this Guide is to assess a student's meaning making. It has two main objectives:

- provide an assessment of the student's level of developmental meaning making in all three dimensions—cognitive, intrapersonal, and interpersonal—as well as an overall assessment of developmental level.
- provide observations on how the student's meaning making influenced his or her experiences and their effects.

In the WNS, we referred to this as the Phase 2 summary. We offer an excerpt of a Phase 2 summary to illustrate this process.

Example of a Phase 2 Summary (Excerpts)

Summary, Phase 2: [Interview ID, Summarizer Name, Date Summary was Completed]

I. Developmental Meaning Making

Overall Meaning Making: Throughout the past year, this student has developed friendships inside and outside of class with peers who are different than her and around whom she feels comfortable being her true self. She attributes her newfound self-awareness to the pledging process for joining the student organization in which she participated. She states:

> "Learning about myself through these [pledge] activities, that was definitely most significant. And quite possibly, that's why I have the friends that I have, because I figured out who I was and we all shared in that experience together." [3]

This student now is able to distinguish how she sees the world, her identity, and her relationships differently than how others—especially her parents—do. Nonetheless, she still feels the pull of her parents' expectations. She notes:

> "I feel like it's hard, too, sometimes. Honestly, one of the biggest struggles here is trying to like stay me and be myself and so, like with my parents' expectations of me, it's hard to be just [student's name] and then be Debutante [student's name] at the same time.

(Continued)

> Balancing that was hard because I really want to be me. I'm really comfortable with me, and my friends know me as who I am, and I figure like I went through like one of the hardest experiences of my life figuring that out. And I hate having to go home like for the summer or for Christmas and not be able to be me." [8]

In essence, this student seems to have an internally defined sense of her identity, relationships, and beliefs yet struggles to express her internal voice when she is with her parents, who seem to exert significant external influences on her. Because the student's internal voice edges out external influences in most settings, her overall meaning-making level is I-E, Listening to the Internal Voice. Nonetheless, she still struggles to block out the noise from her external environment.

Cognitive: This student works to understand contexts in order to determine which knowledge claims are most appropriate and brings her internal voice to the process of deciding what to believe. She explain:

> "Maybe it seems like I'm getting other people's opinions still, but I think that getting information from them, getting their opinions and then even possibly talking to the people that I don't necessarily agree with at first and getting to know their side, why they think that. And then being able to make my own mind up. I think that what it comes down to is knowing yourself and knowing like what you honestly think and being able to support that. And I think that coming into college, I didn't know who I was, so I kind of went along with, 'Well, my friend says that this is how it is, so this is how it is.' And now it's more like, 'I know what I stand for and I know what I'm going to believe, so if it doesn't agree with your opinion, it happens.'" [XSA, 10]

This student not only listens to, but also seeks out different perspectives on topics and then looks inward to make up her own mind. Moreover, she maintains her belief even if others disagree. She adds, "You learn to listen to both sides and then you pick what's best for the situation" [10], which indicates that she does not see only one solution as best for all situations. This student also demonstrates the capacity to integrate and apply knowledge claims. For example, she read Freud's work during the summer and notes:

> "I'm able to draw from it, and pull in conversations, even like today in class. And just being able to relate it, like [it] makes me feel more

(Continued)

I. Developmental Meaning Making (*Continued*)

secure with my understanding and I know that I'm helping other people in the class really lead to something else." [5]

Given her willingness to share insights in class, she seems to recognize her capacity to create knowledge claims and contribute them to a class discussion. Because she no longer uncritically accepts knowledge from her parents and peers and instead looks inward to decide what to believe, she makes meaning in the cognitive dimension at level I(E), Cultivating the Internal Voice. The student's internal voice is present but not fully cultivated, as evidenced in part by her choice to remain quiet when her father shares a perspective about the neighborhood in which she lives with which she disagrees. [7]

Intrapersonal: As this student "pledged" a student organization, she seems to have actively engaged in reflection regarding who she is and made purposeful decisions to align her beliefs and actions with her authentic sense of self. Her friends from college who accept her for who she is have helped her develop her internally defined identity. Reflecting on her first year of college, she explains that she and her friends in high school "weren't always the most sincere people to each other" [2], which led this student to be surprised to find friends in college who are genuine. She adds:

"I think that just finding people who base [friendship] off their feelings toward you based on who you are and not your family was a pleasant surprise, obviously, but that was the biggest surprise for me." [2]

As a result of discovering who she is as compared with who her parents expect her to be, this student chose to change her perspective of others who are different than she is because she believes she must become more open-minded to be an effective elementary school teacher. She states:

"But it's also, it had to happen . . . it's not like I did it cause I just wanted to change. Some people just need to change something one day; they'll go and dye their hair or something. Like, it had to happen. I really don't think that I can be successful as an elementary teacher being close-minded about people . . . If I'm close-minded about one student who decides that she wants to wear all black and not match one day, I can't judge her for that. I still have to be able to nurture her and guide her through her education process. So, it has to happen." [8]

This student demonstrates a firm commitment to staying true to her own beliefs and values such as being open-minded even though her parents have other plans for her. Discussing how she maintains this commitment, she states:

(Continued)

> "It just comes down to respecting myself and realizing how hard I
> worked and how much I went through to get to where I am. And real-
> izing that you know I'm not the girl who hasn't heard of Freud or has-
> n't been witness to different cultures and things like that. I don't know.
> I guess it's just realizing that and confirming that in the head." [8]

In making important decisions such as whether to transfer to another institution, this student works to weigh her priorities yet still needs support from her peers
to follow through on what she decides. [6] Moreover, she continues to experience
tension when her decision conflicts with her parents' expectations. For example,
she concedes that it "kind of sucks" that her parents have different ideas than she
does about whom she should date. [8] Because she is able to maintain internal
commitments in the face of external pressures yet still feels weighed down by
external pressures, her intrapersonal meaning-making level is I(E), Cultivating the
Internal Voice.

Interpersonal: This student works hard to not only remain open to but also learn
from individuals who are different than she is. For example, discussing how her visit
to her friend's hometown in Pennsylvania affected her, she explains, "I think I
learned a lot about my priorities and what I've been taught that has to be my priorities may not always be what's necessary" [1]; in particular, she realized that a
theater production can be just as valuable a source of education as a math text-
book. In addition, although she was initially skeptical of a woman in her English
course who dressed in all black and had pink hair, she realized that she could learn
a great deal from her. The student explains:

> "I was impressed a lot with the fact that she could draw on other
> works of literature or other experiences that she'd had through
> reading these books. And I felt that if I could do that as well, I'd be
> a stronger student." [5]

Ultimately, the student's relationship with this woman—whom she initially dis-
counted as unable to teach her anything—helped her see the value of building
mutually beneficial relationships with diverse others. This student also learned how
to build mutually beneficial relationships during the pledge process. She states:

> "I think that just knowing that I'm being relied upon by other girls
> and knowing that they're going to be there to support me through
> it too, like it just taught me like, you know put in more effort and

(Continued)

I. Developmental Meaning Making (*Continued*)

don't be afraid to do more than just you know your minimum or what you feel like doing that day." [3]

During her first year, this student initially struggled to bring her authentic self to relationships and showed concern for what others thought of her. When she felt other students were gossiping about her due to her prior interactions with a [name of college] student, she felt the need to try to change people's minds about her; she notes that this experience was challenging for her because she was not secure being herself with everybody. [4] She also found it challenging to be "the bottom of the totem pole" because she was used to being "pretty much like the top of [her] high school like, social ladder." [6] In essence, she was used to having the approval of others in high school and did not feel like she enjoyed the same degree of approval in college. This demonstrates that she initially based her relationships on others' reactions. Yet, as she began to interact with others in her classes and in her [college] neighborhood—an area in which she was not allowed to go when she was growing up and in which she and her roommates differ from many of the other families in terms of social class [7]—she began to recognize that she judged people at face-value and then sought to change this. Discussing the impact of these experiences, the student states:

> "I think a lot of people tend to judge like really easily. And I think that just learning not to do that is real important and being open to different people and trying to learn what I can from them, from their culture." [5]

She seems to still struggle to respect those from a lower social class than her own given that her parents place such a high value on maintaining a high social status [7], but she is willing to suspend judgment until she learns more about the individual or culture. Ultimately, external influences still edge out the student's internal voice in terms of interpersonal maturity, but both external and internal voices are present. Thus, her level of interpersonal development is E-I, Constructing the Internal Voice.

II. Summarizer Observations: Links Between Development and Experiences

1. Visiting Pennsylvania
2. Living in [college town]
3. Social Encounter in "Why Read?" Course

(Continued)

II. Summarizer Observations: Links Between Development and Experiences (*Continued*)

Although the student (and the Phase I summarizer) addresses each of these significant experiences separately, I have chosen to combine them here because they interrelate and culminate to create a developmental effect. In essence, each of these experiences exposes the student to perspectives and individuals that are different than those with which she grew up. In particular, when the student visited Pennsylvania, she realized that "southern California lifestyle isn't the only way" and "you can learn things from other sources [such as theater productions] that you didn't expect." [1]

Similarly, by living in an area of [college town] in which she was not allowed to go as a child, she interacts with individuals from different social classes than her own and again realizes that her way of life is not the only way. From a woman in her "Why Read?" course, she realizes that individuals who have a different style and perspective than her own can make valuable contributions to class. Thus, these three experiences—when combined—create enough dissonance to cause the student to question her own perspective and refrain from judging others based on the beliefs and values she inherited from her parents. She explains:

> "I think coming here and seeing so many different cultures represented. . . . It's just like cultures and learning to adjust my values and what I know to what really is." [5]

Rather than dismiss other perspectives and people who appear to hold different values than she does, this student now strives to learn from new ideas and interactions with diverse others. In fact, she sees this as imperative for her career because she believes she cannot be an effective elementary school teacher if she is close-minded. [8] Ultimately, it is difficult to distinguish the developmental impact of each of these experiences on its own, but together, they helped the student grow cognitively and interpersonally. In terms of cognitive development, the student now has the capability to recognize a variety of cultural practices and values as valid whereas she previously saw her own way of life as the only valid way. In terms of interpersonal development, she has moved from seeing perspectives of individuals who are different from her as wrong to refraining from judging others' perspectives before understanding them.

Summary judgment: Developmentally effective experience.

(Continued)

III. Quotations Referenced Above

[Verbatim statements from the interview transcript would be listed here to provide the broader context for the illustrative quotes used above.]

One important lesson learned from training WNS summarizers was that having a firm understanding of principles of human development and the constructive-developmental tradition (summarized in the first chapter of this monograph), bolstered by an understanding of specific student development theories, is essential for this task. For WNS purposes, we offered several resources for summarizers to consult as they prepared for summarizing. These included: Baxter Magolda (2001b—Figure 2.1, Four Phases of the Journey Toward Self-Authorship; 2009a—Table 1.1, Key Locations in the Journey toward Self-Authorship), King and Baxter Magolda (2005—Table 1, A Three-Dimensional Developmental Trajectory of Intercultural Maturity), and Torres and Hernandez (2007—Figure 1, Matrix of Holistic Development Including Latino/a Cultural Choices). In addition to providing summaries of key developmental findings and illustrations of basic developmental principles, these charts offered a quick visual reference for summarizers to use as needed to focus their attention on development within the three dimensions and across the external to internal continuum of self-evolution. A reference list of additional scholarly work on self-authorship development was updated annually and distributed to summarizers as resources they could consult to clarify their understanding. (These are referenced in the first two chapters of this monograph.)

This section of the summary includes the summarizer's assessment of the student's meaning-making structure (the most salient developmental position) on each of the three dimensions (cognitive, intrapersonal, and interpersonal), as well as of the student's overall approach to meaning making. We recommend making this assessment holistically through a careful reading of the whole transcript rather than by conducting a unit-by-unit (or experience-by-experience) analysis.

Considering your own values and assumptions when interpreting developmental level is crucial. We recommend that summarizers identify and carefully review their own sensitizing concepts. These refer to "preconceptions that emanate from such standpoints as class, race, gender, age, embodiment, and historical era [and] may permeate an analysis without the researcher's awareness" (Charmaz, 2006, p. 67). These preconceptions may mediate what one focuses on when reading the transcript (such as those with which you are emotionally engaged) and subsequently affect interpretations of the data. These include assumptions about the purpose of college and the importance (or not) of student organizations in meeting this purpose, the role of parents (for example, worries about "helicopter parents"), assumptions that reflect an investment in selected outcomes (for example, that critical thinking or leadership is most important) or institutional practices (for example, that first-year experience programs are essential), assumptions about learning that vary by institutional size or type, or assumptions about how best instructional practices vary by gender, ethnicity, and other characteristics. Generally the more familiar you are with your own underlying assumptions and can name them, the more likely you are to recognize when they are affecting your interpretations. The goal here is not to eliminate sensitizing concepts (that is likely impossible) but to identify and manage them. In order to do this, you need to be able to make your assumptions object, be willing to own and disclose them to other researchers, and suspend the inclination to use them unreflexively in order to listen to the data. In these ways, the task of constructing summaries requires maturity in cognitive, intrapersonal, and interpersonal dimensions.

There are many ways to manage one's sensitizing concepts while constructing meaning-making assessments. A good starting point is to carefully scrutinize their sources and ask yourself whether these are appropriately applied to this student in this context. Also, remember to finish reading the whole transcript before making an initial assessment in order to put "hot button" comments in context. It is also helpful to ask another summarizer who is familiar with your sensitizing concepts to review your assessment with an eye toward their possible effects on an assessment. Each of these steps (among many other possibilities) helps summarizers approach the process of interpreting meaning making through the eyes of the student who is sharing his or her experiences to best reflect his or her perspective.

In making these assessments, it is important to consider students' comments in the context of the whole transcript; this helps avoid taking a single comment out of context and overinterpreting selected comments. It is also very important to conscientiously and consistently look beneath behavior to the meaning of the student's perspectives. This is key to basing the assessment on structure of meaning making rather than the content of the comments or the experiences.

In the case of multiple (or conflicting) possible assessments, ask yourself, "What is the essence of the meaning making?" and, "Which quotes might supersede other quotes?" For example, if two quotes seem to indicate different meaning making, is it possible to understand both from one meaning-making perspective? If not, does one set of quotes more clearly capture the meaning making? If you remain conflicted about your assessment, record your thoughts and request a consultation with another summarizer.

Once you have arrived at an assessment, write several descriptive sentences or a short paragraph summarizing your assessment, illustrating your conclusions and observations with verbatim examples. Choose illustrative quotes that most clearly illustrate the developmental meaning-making level in the student's own words and show the basis for your assessments about this student's experience. These examples give you the opportunity to select and offer the best evidence from the transcript in support of your observations. When inserting a quote, add background contextual information if this is not part of the quote itself. For example, you might note what question the student is answering, or what experience, organization, or person he or she is referring to in the quoted passage. Overall, try to be as transparent as possible in your assessment. If you are unsure or struggled with a particular rating, it is appropriate to record that in your summary. This information is helpful for others who engage in later analysis and may also contribute to ongoing efforts to refine the definitions of and distinctions between self-authorship levels.

Organize these quotes into footnotes by using a number in brackets, and cite the footnote number when referencing the quote; assigning a specific number to the quote allows easy retrieval in the future. Use the designation "XSA" to flag exemplary quotes related to meaning-making position; these quotes illustrate a developmental position particularly well. Finally, note other supporting pieces of information located elsewhere in the transcript, along with their location. This also expedites future retrieval if desired in subsequent analysis.

Record each assessment by reference to one or more of the positions on the ten-step meaning-making continuum (see Figure 1). Repeat this process for each dimension and your overall assessment. Conclude this section with a statement on the richness of the data within this transcript. This has an impact on the level of confidence with which we can say that the meaning-making levels were appropriately assessed.

Links Between Development and Experiences

It is helpful for both research and educational purposes to document observed relationships between students' experiences and how they make meaning of the experiences (which reflects their developmental levels). This is particularly important for those who seek to understand or influence what students learn from their experiences. The following step is designed to record any observed links between development and students' experiences.

Review the important experiences in the Phase 1 summary and consider how the student's meaning-making position appeared to influence her or his experience. Note any links you observe regarding how the student's meaning-making position influenced how this student approached, engaged in, or reacted to experiences she or he described. For example, you might note that a student whose meaning making you assessed as Trusting External Authority willingly interacted with diverse peers because she had been brought up to do so, but did not reflect on encountering difference or what it meant for her own identity or understanding multiple perspectives. In contrast, for another student whose meaning making you assessed as Recognizing Shortcomings of Trusting External Authority, you might note that she felt considerable dissonance by encountering those with diverse perspectives and reacted by realizing the need to rethink initial stereotypes about others. These kinds of observations also illustrate the nature and quality of contexts that promote development, the focus of the final step in this process.

Finally, note the experiences you judge to be developmentally effective, that is, those that in your judgment resulted in the student's more complex view of the world, self, or relationships. Your judgment may be informed by an observation shared by the student about how she or he had changed, but must be confirmed by your own assessment of the shift reported by the student. In one or two sentences, specify your reasons for this designation and note the appropriate footnotes that illustrate the more complex view. For example, does the student articulate a subject-object shift? Does she see knowledge, self, others, or the context in more complex ways? If needed, add additional footnotes to those already included in the Phase 2 summary. (For a description of the concepts underlying these questions, see the first chapter of this monograph; for an example of the footnotes, see section II of "Example of a Phase 2 Summary."

Working Through Difficult Summaries

In making your assessments of the meaning-making positions for a student in each of the three dimensions and overall, it is reasonable to expect that you will come across interviews that you find difficult to assess. Remember that your goal as a summarizer is to give your best read of the data presented through the transcript. This section is intended to help you navigate challenging interviews you may encounter.

You may encounter transcripts where the language the student uses seems more advanced than his or her meaning making, that is, the structure does not match the content. Or you may encounter students who exhibit characteristics of two distinct meaning-making positions at different points in the same interview. Be sure to read the interviewer commentary at the end of the transcript before starting your assessment, even if you were the interviewer. The interviewer may have recorded some important information about the conversation that will help figure out a challenging interview. Following are some prompts you can ask yourself as you make your interpretations, as well as some useful language to help you in writing up a difficult summary.

If you are unsure whether the voice you hear in the transcript is externally or internally constructed, ask yourself:

- How did the person arrive at these conclusions?
- What are his or her reasons for holding these beliefs, values, and so on?
- How did the person use sources she or he identified? Uncritical acceptance of others' perspectives indicates an external meaning-making structure; careful consideration of others' perspectives to determine their value indicates an internal meaning-making structure.

Each of these questions is designed to help ground the assessment in the respondent's frame of reference that informs his or her meaning making.

If a person's meaning making in one dimension seems much more developed than in other dimensions, ask yourself:

- Did the individual use buzz words such as *critical thinking* that would bias me in a certain direction?
- What evidence do I have for experiences or factors that spurred growth in one dimension while halting or delaying it in other dimensions?

In all cases, whatever one position you select that best reflects each dimension, make your decision based on your best read of the data and using the illustrative quotes.

Here is some sample language to get you unstuck, clarify your thinking and your overall reactions, and begin writing up the assessment:

- This was a difficult dimension for me to assess because . . .
- I was deciding between Eb and Ec on this dimension because . . .
- Ultimately my decision was based on . . .
- My own subjectivities about X make this transcript challenging for me to assess because. . . .

Finally, if you have sustained difficulties working on a particular summary and the strategies discussed here do not help, we recommend getting some assistance from someone who has deep familiarity with self-evolution theory, developmental assessment, or self-authorship assessment.

The Value of Listening to Students

We recognize that the Guide we offer reflects a time-intensive and complex approach to assessing development, as does the interview process on which it is based. At the same time, we are impressed by the quality of data about meaning making and the development of self-authorship that this approach can yield. This approach has also yielded many insights and examples about the kinds of experiences that promote and inhibit the process of learning to self-author one's life and how powerful experiences occur across a variety of settings, including curricular and cocurricular settings, formal and informal settings, and family and work settings.

We are encouraged that large-scale assessment is possible by organizing and training large assessment teams. Many of the WNS team members were master's or doctoral students who used their involvement to meet research requirements or gain research experience in their program. Many continued with the project after their graduation to further their professional development and contribute to a distinctive research project. This experience suggests that the creative involvement of graduate students and professional staff can boost an institution's assessment efforts, help educators acquire an in-depth understanding of the learners they serve, and form a foundation for practice that promotes the developmental capacities and learning of all involved in this process.

Although the assessment process described here is complex and requires sustained attention, this type of process is essential if the goal is a deep understanding of the way students' underlying assumptions affect how they process what they are learning. Ultimately this understanding can inform the kinds of experiences educators seek to provide and the ways they assess the effectiveness of these experiences. The fact that the process itself demands knowledge, skills, and maturity across developmental domains reflects the holistic approach to educational practices that we have articulated elsewhere (Baxter Magolda, 1999, 2001b; Baxter Magolda and King, 2004, 2008; King and Baxter Magolda, 1996, 2005). A key component of this assessment process builds on a practice that astute educators use: listening to students and seeking to understand the basis for their views and actions (such as approaches to studying, delegating group responsibilities, and making choices about how to interact with friends). Externally defined students may be seeking validation when meeting with a teacher, advisor, or mentor, and those who are unaware of the power of this dynamic may simply tell the student what to do rather than seeing this as an opportunity to help the student learn to become self-authored by exploring and encouraging decision making that is not only well informed but internally grounded. We advocate reflective conversations in which "the key element is encouraging students to make sense of their experience rather than the educators making sense of it for them" (Baxter Magolda and King, 2008, p. 9). These conversations resemble self-authorship interviews in that both encourage deep reflection about students' experiences and provide ways to help students learn from their experiences as they make decisions about the kinds of lives they seek to live and the kinds of people they seek to become. We hope the nuanced portrait of multiple pathways toward self-authorship and the rich narratives that illustrate those possibilities will provide readers a foundation from which to engage effectively in these reflective conversations.

Appendix: Wabash National Study of Liberal Arts Education: Qualitative Research Team

Many individuals contributed to this project, and their observations and insights collectively shaped our assessment process. Here, we acknowledge the participation and contributions of those who assisted with the collection, analysis, and management of the interview data in both the pilot and the longitudinal assessments:

Carin Barber

James Barber

Cassie Barnhardt

Inger Bergom

Marta Brill

Marie Kendall Brown

Jennifer Buckley

Ariela Canizole

Taran Cardone

Heather Christman

Cherry Danielson

Michael Denton

Julie DeGraw

Amber Dehne

Jenn Dize

Kristy Drobney

Joanna Frye

Holly Gage

Rachael Gebely

Debra Gentry

Lorenzo Gutierrez

Mandy Hart

Melissa Healy

Matthew Holsapple

Aurora Israelson

Cindy Jiang

Kimberly Johnson

Jeongeun Kim

Kim Klein

Lisa Landreman

Jenn Laskowski

Anne Laughlin

Anat Levtov

Matt Lewis

Kim Lijana
Nathan Lindsay
Geisce Ly
Brianne MacEachran
Johanna Masse
Jennifer McLaughlin
Ramona Meraz
Lily Muzame
Kira Pasquesi
Rosemary Perez
Dwayne Peterson
Kate Poisson
Fisher Qua
Kelly Rainey
Michael Rayle
Leah Reynolds Joos
Laura Rhoades

Melinda Richardson
Donna Scheid
Erin Schilling
Tricia Seifert
Laura Shapiro
Andrea Shea
Woojeong Shim
Ruby Siddiqui
Carly Stamey
Ethan Stephenson
Kari Taylor
JoNes VanHecke
Kerri Wakefield
Kelley Walczak
Trist Wdziekonski
Jamie Workman
Joel Zylstra

References

Abes, E. S. (2012). Constructivist and intersectional interpretations of a lesbian college student's multiple social identities. *Journal of Higher Education, 83*(2), 186–216. doi:10.1353/jhe.2012.0013

Abes, E. S., and Jones, S. R. (2004). Meaning-making capacity and the dynamics of lesbian college students' multiple dimensions of identity. *Journal of College Student Development, 45*(6), 612–632.

Abes, E. S., Jones, S. R., and McEwen, M. K. (2007). Reconceptualizing the model of multiple dimensions of identity: The role of meaning-making capacity in the construction of multiple identities. *Journal of College Student Development, 48*(1), 1–22.

Abes, E. S., and Kasch, D. (2007). Using queer theory to explore lesbian college students' multiple dimensions of identity. *Journal of College Student Development, 48*(6), 619–636.

Accrediting Board for Engineering and Technology. (2012). *Criteria for accrediting engineering programs, 2012–2013.* Accrediting Board for Engineering and Technology. http://www.abet.org/engineering-criteria-2012-2013/.

Accrediting Council for Independent Colleges and Schools. (2011a). *Closing the gap.* White paper. Washington, DC: Accrediting Council for Independent Colleges and Schools.

Accrediting Council for Independent Colleges and Schools. (2011b) *ACICS research fact sheet.* Washington, DC: Accrediting Council for Independent Colleges and Schools.

American Association of Colleges and Universities. (2002). *Greater expectations: A new vision for learning as a nation goes to college.* Washington, DC: American Association of Colleges and Universities.

Arum, R., and Roksa, J. (2011). *Academically adrift: Limited learning on college campuses.* Chicago: University of Chicago Press.

Baxter Magolda, M. B. (1987). A comparison of open-ended interview and standardized instrument measures of intellectual development on the Perry scheme. *Journal of College Student Personnel, 28*, 443–448.

Baxter Magolda, M. B. (1992). *Knowing and reasoning in college: Gender-related patterns in students' intellectual development.* San Francisco: Jossey-Bass.

Baxter Magolda, M. B. (1999). *Creating contexts for learning and self-authorship: Constructive-developmental pedagogy.* Nashville, TN: Vanderbilt University Press.

Baxter Magolda, M. B. (2001a). A constructivist revision of the measure of epistemological reflection. *Journal of College Student Development, 42*(6), 520–534.

Baxter Magolda, M. B. (2001b). *Making their own way: Narratives for transforming higher education to promote self-development.* Sterling, VA: Stylus.

Baxter Magolda, M. B. (2004). Learning partnerships model: A framework for promoting self-authorship. In M. B. Baxter Magolda and P. M. King (Eds.), *Learning partnerships: Theory and models of practice to educate for self-authorship* (pp. 37–62). Sterling, VA: Stylus.

Baxter Magolda, M. B. (2008). Three elements of self-authorship. *Journal of College Student Development, 49*(4), 269–284.

Baxter Magolda, M. B. (2009a). *Authoring your life: Developing an internal voice to navigate life's challenges.* Sterling, VA: Stylus.

Baxter Magolda, M. B. (2009b). The activity of meaning making: A holistic perspective on college student development. *Journal of College Student Development, 50*(6), 621–639.

Baxter Magolda, M. B. (2010). Future directions: Pursuing theoretical and methodological issues in the evolution of self-authorship. In M. B. Baxter Magolda, E. G. Creamer, and P. S. Meszaros (Eds.), *Development and assessment of self-authorship: Exploring the concept across cultures* (pp. 267–284). Sterling, VA: Stylus.

Baxter Magolda, M. B., and King, P. M. (Eds.). (2004). *Learning partnerships: Theory and models of practice to educate for self-authorship.* Sterling, VA: Stylus.

Baxter Magolda, M. B., and King, P. M. (2007). Interview strategies for assessing self-authorship: Constructing conversations to assess meaning making. *Journal of College Student Development, 48*(5), 491–508.

Baxter Magolda, M. B., and King, P. M. (2008). Toward reflective conversations: An advising approach that promotes self-authorship. *Peer Review, 10*(1) 8–11.

Baxter Magolda, M. B., King, P. M., and Drobney, K. L. (2010). Practices that provide effective academic challenge for first-year students. *Journal on Excellence in College Teaching, 21*(2), 45–65.

Baxter Magolda, M. B., King, P. M., Taylor, K. B., and Perez, R. J. (2008, November). *Developmental steps within external meaning making.* Paper presented at the annual meeting of the Association for the Study of Higher Education, Jacksonville, FL.

Baxter Magolda, M. B., King, P. M., Taylor, K. B., and Wakefield, K. (2012). Decreasing authority dependence during the first year of college. *Journal of College Student Development, 53*(3), 418–435.

Baxter Magolda, M. B., and Porterfield, W. D. (1985). A new approach to assess intellectual development on the Perry scheme. *Journal of College Student Personnel, 26*, 343–351.

Baxter Magolda, M. B., and Porterfield, W. D. (1988). *Assessing intellectual development: The link between theory and practice.* Alexandria, VA: American College Personnel Association.

Belenky, M., Clinchy, B. M., Goldberger, N., and Tarule, J. (1986). *Women's ways of knowing: The development of self, voice, and mind.* New York: Basic Books.

Berger, J. G. (2010). Using the subject-object interview to promote and assess self-authorship. In M. B. Baxter Magolda, E. G. Creamer, and P. S. Meszaros (Eds.), *Development and assessment of self-authorship: Exploring the concept across cultures* (pp. 245–264). Sterling, VA: Stylus.

Boes, L. M., Baxter Magolda, M. B., and Buckley, J. A. (2010). Foundational assumptions and constructive-developmental theory: Self-authorship narratives. In M. B. Baxter Magolda, E. G. Creamer, and P. S. Meszaros (Eds.), *Development and assessment of self-authorship: Exploring the concept across cultures* (pp. 3–23). Sterling, VA: Stylus.

Charmaz, K. (2003). Qualitative interviewing and grounded theory analysis. In J. A. Holstein and J. F. Gubrium (Eds.), *Inside interviewing: New lenses, new concerns* (pp. 311–330). Thousand Oaks, CA: Sage.

Charmaz, K. C. (2006). *Constructing grounded theory: A practical guide through qualitative analysis.* Thousand Oaks, CA: Sage.

Clandinin, D. J., and Connelly, F. M. (2000). *Narrative inquiry: Experience and story in qualitative research.* San Francisco: Jossey-Bass.

Creamer, E. G., Baxter Magolda, M. B., and Yue, J. (2010). Preliminary evidence of the reliability and validity of a quantitative measure of self-authorship. *Journal of College Student Development, 51*(5), 550–562.

Creamer, E. G., and Laughlin, A. (2005). Self-authorship and women's career decision making. *Journal of College Student Development, 46*(1), 13–27.

Dunbar, C., Jr., Rodriguez, D., and Parker, L. (2003). Race, subjectivity, and the interview process. In J. A. Holstein and J. F. Gubrium (Eds.), *Inside interviewing: New lenses, new concerns* (pp. 131–150). Thousand Oaks, CA: Sage.

Fischer, K. W. (1980). A theory of cognitive development: The control and construction of hierarchies of skill. *Psychological Review, 87*, 477–531.

Gibbs, J., and Widaman, K. F. (1982). *Social intelligence: Measuring the development of sociomoral reflection.* Englewood Cliffs, NJ: Prentice Hall.

Gibbs, J. C., and others. (1984). Construction and validation of a multiple-choice measure of moral reasoning. *Child Development, 55*, 527–536.

Gilligan, C. (1982). *In a different voice.* Cambridge, MA: Harvard University Press.

Goodman, K., and Seifert, T. (2009, April). *The process of developing a brief survey of self-authorship.* Paper presented at the American Educational Research Association, San Diego, CA.

Hahn, I. G. (1991). *The role of domain predominance and its relationship with utilization in moral decision-making.* Unpublished doctoral dissertation, University of Wisconsin–Madison.

Heifetz, R. (1998). *Leadership without easy answers.* Cambridge, MA: Harvard University Press.

Holstein, J. A., and Gubrium, J. F. (2003). Active interviewing. In J. F. Gubrium and J. A. Holstein (Eds.), *Postmodern interviewing* (pp. 67–80). Thousand Oaks, CA: Sage.

Hunt, D. E., and Sullivan, E. V. (1974). *Between psychology and education.* Hillsdale, IL: Dryden Press.

Ignelzi, M. (2000). Meaning-making in the learning and teaching process. In M. B. Baxter Magolda (Ed.), *Teaching to promote intellectual and personal maturity: Incorporating students' worldviews and identities into the learning process.* New Directions for Teaching and Learning (Vol. 82, pp. 5–14). San Francisco: Jossey-Bass.

Jordan, J. V. (1997). A relational perspective for understanding women's development. In J. V. Jordan (Ed.), *Women's growth in diversity: More writings from the Stone Center* (pp. 9–24). New York: Guilford Press.

Keeling, R. P. (Ed.). (2004). *Learning reconsidered: A campus-wide focus on the student experience.* Washington DC: National Association of Student Personnel Administrators and American College Personnel Association.

Kegan, R. (1982). *The evolving self: Problem and process in human development.* Cambridge, MA: Harvard University Press.

Kegan, R. (1994). *In over our heads: The mental demands of modern life.* Cambridge, MA: Harvard University Press.

Kegan, R. (2000). What "form" transforms? A constructive-developmental approach to transformative learning. In J. Mezirow (Ed.), *Learning as transformation: Critical perspectives on a theory in progress* (pp. 35–69). San Francisco: Jossey-Bass.

Kegan, R., and Lahey, L. L. (2009). *Immunity to change: How to overcome it and unlock potential in yourself and your organization.* Boston: Harvard Business School Press.

King, P. M. (1990). Assessing development from a cognitive-developmental perspective. In D. Creamer and Associates (Eds.), *College student development: Theory and practice for the 1990s* (pp. 81–98). Alexandria, VA: American College Personnel Association.

King, P. M. (2009). Principles of development and developmental change underlying theories of cognitive and moral development. *Journal of College Student Development, 50*(6), 597–639.

King, P. M. (2010). The role of the cognitive dimension of self-authorship: An equal partner or the strong partner? In M. B. Baxter Magolda, E. G. Creamer, and P. S. Meszaros (Eds.), *Development and assessment of self-authorship: Exploring the concept across cultures* (pp. 167–185). Sterling, VA: Stylus.

King, P. M., and Baxter Magolda, M. B. (1996). A developmental perspective on learning. *Journal of College Student Development, 37*(2), 163–173.

King, P. M., and Baxter Magolda, M. B. (2005). A developmental model of intercultural maturity. *Journal of College Student Development, 46*(6), 571–592.

King, P. M., Baxter Magolda, M. B., and Masse, J. (2011). Maximizing learning from engaging across difference: The role of anxiety and meaning-making. *Equity and Excellence in Education, 44*(4), 468–487.

King, P. M., Baxter Magolda, M. B., Perez, R. J., and Taylor, K. B. (2009, November). *Refining the journey toward self-authorship: Developmental steps within the crossroads.* Paper presented at the annual meeting of the Association for the Study of Higher Education, Vancouver, BC.

King, P. M., Kendall Brown, M., Lindsay, N. K., and VanHecke, J. R. (2007). Liberal arts student learning outcomes: An integrated approach. *About Campus: Enriching the Student Learning Experience, 12*(4), 2–9.

King, P. M., and Kitchener, K. S. (1994). *Developing reflective judgment: Understanding and promoting intellectual growth and critical thinking in adolescents and adults.* San Francisco: Jossey-Bass.

King, P. M., and Kitchener, K. S. (2004). Reflective judgment: Theory and research on the development of epistemic assumptions through adulthood. *Educational Psychologist, 39*(1), 5–18.

King, P. M., and Siddiqui, R. (2011). Self-authorship and metacognition: Related constructs for understanding college student learning and development. In C. Hoare (Ed.), *The Oxford handbook of reciprocal adult development and learning* (pp. 113–131). New York: Oxford University Press.

King, P. M., and VanHecke, J. (2006). Making connections: Using skill theory to recognize how students build—and rebuild—understanding. *About Campus: Enhancing the Student Learning Experience, 11*(1), 10–16.

King, P. M., and others. (2009). Developmentally effective experiences for promoting self-authorship. *Mind, Brain, and Education, 3*(2), 108–118.

Kitchener, K. S., Lynch, C. L., Fischer, K. W., and Wood, P. K. (1993). Developmental range of reflective judgment: The effect of contextual support and practice on developmental stage. *Developmental Psychology, 29*(5), 893–906.

Knefelkamp, L. (1974). *Development instruction: Fostering intellectual and personal growth of college students.* Dissertation, University of Minnesota, Minneapolis.

Kohlberg, L. (1984). *Essays on moral development, Vol. 1. The philosophy of moral development.* New York: HarperCollins.

Kroll, B. (1992). Reflective inquiry in a college English class. *Liberal Education, 78*(1), 10–13.

Kuhn, D., and Dean, D., Jr. (2004). Metacognition: A bridge between cognitive psychology and educational practice. *Theory into Practice, 43*(4), 268–273.

Kvale, S. (1996). *Interviews: An introduction to qualitative research interviewing.* Thousand Oaks, CA: Sage.

Lahey, L. L., and others. (1988). *A guide to the subject-object interview: Its administration and interpretation*: Cambridge, MA: Subject-Object Research Group.

Lamborn, S. D., and Fischer, K. W. (1988). Optimal and functional levels in cognitive development: The individual's developmental range. *Newsletter of the International Society for the Study of Behavioral Development, 2*(14), 1–4.

Laughlin, A., and Creamer, E. G. (2007). Engaging differences: Self-authorship and the decision making process. In P. S. Meszaros (Ed.), *Self-authorship: Advancing students' intellectual growth.* New Directions for Teaching and Learning (Vol. 109, pp. 43–51). San Francisco: Jossey Bass.

Mentkowski, M., and Associates. (2000). *Learning that lasts: Integrating learning, development, and performance in college and beyond.* San Francisco: Jossey-Bass.

Mezirow, J. (1997). Transformative learning: Theory to practice. In P. Cranton (Ed.), *Transformative learning in action: Insights from practice.* New Directions for Adult and Continuing Education (Vol. 74, pp. 5–12). San Francisco: Jossey-Bass.

Moore, W. S. (1989). The learning environment preferences: Exploring the construct validity of an objective measure of the Perry scheme of intellectual development. *Journal of College Student Development, 30,* 504–514.

Pascarella, E. T., Blaich, C., Martin, G. L., and Hanson, J. M. (2011). How robust are the findings of *Academically Adrift? Change, 43*(3), 20–24.

Pascarella, E. T., and Terenzini, P. T. (1991). *How college affects students: Findings and insights from twenty years of research.* San Francisco: Jossey-Bass.

Pascarella, E. T., and Terenzini, P. T. (2005). *How college affects students: A third decade of research.* San Francisco: Jossey-Bass.

Patton, M. Q. (2001). *Qualitative research and evaluation methods.* (3rd ed.) Thousand Oaks, CA: Sage.

Perez, R. J., Shim, W., King, P. M., and Baxter Magolda, M. B. (2011, November). *Mapping developmental shifts in intercultural maturity among college students.* Paper presented at the Association for the Study of Higher Education, Charlotte, NC.

Perry, W. G. (1970). *Forms of intellectual and ethical development in the college years: A scheme.* Troy, MO: Holt.

Piaget, J. (1948). *The moral judgment of the child.* New York: Free Press.

Piaget, J. (1950). *The psychology of intelligence* (M. Piercy and D. Berlyne, Trans.). London: Routledge.

Pizzolato, J. E. (2003). Developing self-authorship: Exploring the experiences of high-risk college students. *Journal of College Student Development, 44*(6), 797–812.

Pizzolato, J. E. (2004). Coping with conflict: Self-authorship, coping, and adaptation to college in first-year, high-risk students. *Journal of College Student Development, 45*(4), 425–442.

Pizzolato, J. E. (2005). Creating crossroads for self-authorship: Investigating the provocative moment. *Journal of College Student Development, 46*(6), 624–641.

Pizzolato, J. E. (2007a). Assessing self-authorship. In P. S. Meszaros (Ed.), *Self-authorship: Advancing students' intellectual growth.* New Directions for Teaching and Learning (Vol., 109, pp. 31–42). San Francisco: Jossey-Bass.

Pizzolato, J. E. (2007b). Meaning making inside and outside the academic arena: Investigating the contextuality of epistemological development in college students. *Journal of General Education, 56*(3&4), 228–251.

Pizzolato, J. E. (2010). What is self-authorship? A theoretical exploration of the construct. In M. B. Baxter Magolda, E. G. Creamer, and P. S. Meszaros (Eds.), *Development and assessment of self-authorship: Exploring the concept across cultures* (pp. 187–206). Sterling, VA: Stylus.

Pizzolato, J. E., and Chaudhari, P. (2009, April). *Complicating assessment: Considerations for quantitative measurement of self-authorship.* Paper presented at the American Educational Research Association, San Diego, CA.

Rest, J. R. (1979). *Development in judging moral issues.* Minneapolis: University of Minnesota Press.

Rest, J. R., Narváez, D., Bebeau, M. J., and Thoma, S. J. (1999). *Postconventional thinking: A neo-Kohlbergian approach.* Mahwah, NJ: Erlbaum.

Sanford, N. (1962). Developmental status of the entering freshman. In N. Sanford (Ed.), *The American college: A psychological and social interpretation of the higher learning* (pp. 253–282). Hoboken, NJ: Wiley.

Sanford, N. (1966). *Self and society: Social change and individual development.* New York: Atherton.

Schwartz, M. S., and Fischer, K. W. (2006). Useful metaphors for tackling problems in teaching and learning. *About Campus: Enriching the Student Learning Experience, 11*(1), 2–9.

Seifert, T., Goodman, K., King, P. M., and Baxter Magolda, M. B. (2010). Using mixed methods to study first-year college impact on liberal arts learning outcomes. *Journal of Mixed Method Research, 4*(3), 248–267.

Taylor, K. B. (2008). Mapping the intricacies of young adults' developmental journey from socially prescribed to internally defined identities, relationships, and beliefs. *Journal of College Student Development, 49*(3), 215–234.

Tharp, R. G., and Gallimore, R. (1988). *Rousing minds to life: Teaching, learning, and schooling in social context.* Cambridge: Cambridge University Press.

Thoma, S. J. (2002). An overview of the Minnesota approach to research in moral development. *Journal of Moral Education, 31*(3), 225–245.

Thoma, S. J., and Rest, J. R. (1999). The relationship between moral decision making and patterns of consolidation and transition in moral judgment development. *Developmental Psychology, 35*(2), 323–334.

Thoma, S. J., Rest, J. R., and Davison, M. L. (1991). Describing and testing a moderator of the moral judgment and action relationship. *Journal of Personality and Social Psychology, 61*, 659–669.

Torres, V. (2009). The developmental dimensions of recognizing racist thoughts. *Journal of College Student Development, 50*(5), 504–520.

Torres, V. (2010). Investigating Latino ethnic identity within the self-authorship framework. In M. B. Baxter Magolda, E. G. Creamer, and P. S. Meszaros (Eds.), *Development and assessment of self-authorship: Exploring the concept across cultures* (pp. 67–84). Sterling, VA: Stylus.

Torres, V., and Baxter Magolda, M. B. (2004). Reconstructing Latino identity: The influence of cognitive development on the ethnic identity process of Latino students. *Journal of College Student Development, 45*(3), 333–347.

Torres, V., and Hernandez, E. (2007). The influence of ethnic identity development on self-authorship: A longitudinal study of Latino/a college students. *Journal of College Student Development, 48*(5), 558–573.

Walker, L. J., and Taylor, J. H. (1991). Stage transitions in moral reasoning: A longitudinal study of developmental processes. *Developmental Psychology, 27*, 330–337.

Weiss, R. S. (1994). *Learning from strangers: The art and method of qualitative interview studies.* New York: Free Press.

Widick, C. (1975). *An evaluation of developmental instruction in a university setting.* Dissertation, University of Minnesota, Minneapolis.

Wildman, T. M. (2007). Taking seriously the intellectual growth of students: Accommodations for self-authorship. In P. S. Meszaros (Ed.), *Self-authorship: Advancing students' intellectual growth.* New Directions for Teaching and Learning (Vol. 109, pp. 15–30). San Francisco: Jossey-Bass.

Wood, P., Kitchener, K. S., and Jensen, L. (2002). Considerations in the design and evaluation of a paper-and-pencil measure of epistemic cognition. In B. K. Hofer and P. R. Pintrich (Eds.), *Personal epistemology: The psychology of beliefs about knowledge and knowing* (pp. 277–294). Mahwah, NJ: Erlbaum.

Name Index

A
Abes, E. S., 9, 14, 23, 24
Arum, R., 2

B
Barber, J. P., 37, 46
Baxter Magolda, M. B., 3, 5, 6, 9, 13–16,
    22–28, 31–34, 37–39, 40, 44, 46, 48,
    49, 51, 68, 71, 72, 82, 83, 85–95, 98,
    101, 102, 113, 119, 120
Bebeau, M. J., 9
Belenky, M., 23–24, 38
Berger, J. G., 23–25, 28–32, 38
Blaich, C., 2–3
Boes, L. M., 6
Buckley, J. A., 6

C
Charmaz, K. C., 39, 45, 114
Chaudhari, P., 27–28
Clandinin, D. J., 39
Clinchy, B. M., 23–24, 38
Connelly, F. M., 39
Creamer, E. G., 27

D
Davison, M. L., 9
Dean, D., Jr., 12
Drobney, K. L., 3
Dunbar, C., Jr., 44

F
Fischer, K. W., 7, 10–11, 24–25

G
Gallimore, R., 2
Gibbs, J., 22, 25–26
Gilligan, C., 22–24
Goldberger, N., 23–24, 38
Goodman, K., 28, 40
Gubrium, J. F., 44

H
Hahn, I. G., 9–10
Hanson, J. M., 2–3
Heifetz, R., 19
Hernandez, E., 9, 14, 24, 49, 113
Holstein, J. A., 44
Hunt, D. E., 2

I
Ignelzi, M., 48

J
Jensen, L., 26, 27
Jones, S. R., 9, 14, 23, 24
Jordan, J. V., 23–24

K
Kasch, D., 9, 14, 24

Subject Index

D

Defining Issues Test (Rest), 26
Developmentalism, 7–11
Diana (case illustration), 78–83
Disequilibrium (term; Piaget), 8–9

E

Ea. *See* Trusting External Authority (Ea)
Eb. *See* Tensions with Trusting External
    Authority (Eb)
Ec. *See* Recognizing Shortcomings of
    Trusting External authority position
    (Ec)
E(I). *See* Questioning External Authority
    [E(I)]
E-I. *See*Constructing the Internal Voice
    (E-I)
Epistemological (term), 5
Epistemological Reflection Interview
    (Baxter Magolda), 31, 101
Evan (case illustration), 88–90, 94-97
External Formulas, 27
External influences, 13, 14
External meaning making, developmental
    progression in, 65–66
External positions: and entering crossroads,
    67–73; predominantly, (entering
    crossroads), 67–73; and Recognizing
    Shortcomings of Trusting External
    Authority (Ec), 53–54; and Tensions
    with Trusting External Authority (Eb),
    53; and Trusting External Authority
    (Ea), 53
External positions, predominantly: and
    Constructing the Internal Voice (E-I),
    73–76; and Questioning External
    Authority [E(I)], 67–76

F

Following External Formulas approach, 13,
    39–40

G

Gavin (case illustration), 55–61
GrowthEdge Interview (Berger), 23, 28–31

H

Habits of mind, 7
Helicopter parents, 114

I

Ia. *See* Trusting the Internal Voice (Ia)
Ib. *See* Building an Internal Foundation
    (Ib)
Ic. *See* Securing Internal Commitments (Ic)
I(E). *See* Cultivating the Internal Voice
    [I(E)]
I-E. *See* Listening to the Internal Voice
"Immunity to change" (Kegan and Lahey),
    7
Internal meaning making, developmental
    progression in, 98–99
Internal positions, predominantly, 77–86;
    and Cultivating the Internal Voice
    [I(E)], 78–86; and Listening to the
    Internal Voice (I-E), 77–78
Internal voice, 14; Constructing (E-1),
    73–76; Cultivating [I(E)], 78–86;
    Listening to (I-E), 77–78; seeing need
    for, 72–73; Trusting (Ia), 88–90
Iraq, war in, 60

J

Justine (case illustration), 68–71, 73-74

K

Kerry (case illustration), 96, 97

L

Lauren (case illustration), 71, 72, 74-76
Learning Environment Preferences
    (Moore), 27
Listening to the Internal Voice (I-E),
    77–78, 83, 85

M

Meaning making: and collegiate learning
    outcomes, 4–5; concept of, 6;
    constructivism and, 6–7; developmental
    progression in external meaning making,
    65–66; developmental progression in

About the Authors

Marcia B. Baxter Magolda is Distinguished Professor of Educational Leadership at Miami University of Ohio. She received her Ph.D. and M.A. in higher education from the Ohio State University and her B.A. in psychology from Capital University. She teaches student development theory and research in the Student Affairs in Higher Education master's and doctoral programs. Her scholarship addresses the evolution of learning and development in college and young adult life and pedagogy to promote self-authorship. She has authored three books on her twenty-five-year longitudinal study of adult development: *Authoring Your Life*, *Making Their Own Way*, and *Knowing and Reasoning in College*. She is the author or coeditor of six additional books. She is a co–principal investigator on the Wabash National Study of Liberal Arts Education (www.soe.umich.edu/liberalartstudy). She has received the Association for the Study of Higher Education Research Achievement Award, the National Association of Student Personnel Administrators' Robert H. Shaffer Award for Excellence as a Graduate Faculty Member, the American College Personnel Association's Contribution to Knowledge Award, and Miami University's Benjamin Harrison Medallion.

Patricia M. King is a Professor of Higher Education in the Center for the Study of Higher and Postsecondary Education at the University of Michigan. Her teaching and research focus on the learning and development of late adolescents and adults, especially college students. She is interested in approaches to development that explore the intersections among developmental domains, such as intellectual, identity, and social development, and how these affect a range of collegiate outcomes, such as intercultural maturity, citizenship, and character development. Her current work focuses on the development of self-authorship, especially as it relates to learning outcomes in postsecondary settings. She is a co–principal investigator on the Wabash National Study of Liberal Arts Education (www.soe.umich.edu/liberalartstudy). She has co-authored two books: *Developing Reflective Judgment* (with Karen Strohm Kitchener) and *Learning Partnerships: Theory and Models of Practice to Educate for Self-Authorship* (with Marcia Baxter Magolda). She served as the founding editor of *About Campus: Enriching the Student Learning Experience*, the national magazine sponsored by the American College Personnel Association. She has served on several advisory boards for the American Association of Colleges and Universities, including the Research and Educational Change Collaborative, part of the Educating for Personal and Social Responsibility Project.

About the ASHE Higher Education Report Series

Since 1983, the ASHE (formerly ASHE-ERIC) Higher Education Report Series has been providing researchers, scholars, and practitioners with timely and substantive information on the critical issues facing higher education. Each monograph presents a definitive analysis of a higher education problem or issue, based on a thorough synthesis of significant literature and institutional experiences. Topics range from planning to diversity and multiculturalism, to performance indicators, to curricular innovations. The mission of the Series is to link the best of higher education research and practice to inform decision making and policy. The reports connect conventional wisdom with research and are designed to help busy individuals keep up with the higher education literature. Authors are scholars and practitioners in the academic community. Each report includes an executive summary, review of the pertinent literature, descriptions of effective educational practices, and a summary of key issues to keep in mind to improve educational policies and practice.

The Series is one of the most peer reviewed in higher education. A National Advisory Board made up of ASHE members reviews proposals. A National Review Board of ASHE scholars and practitioners reviews completed manuscripts. Six monographs are published each year and they are approximately 144 pages in length. The reports are widely disseminated through Jossey-Bass and John Wiley & Sons, and they are available online to subscribing institutions through Wiley Online Library (http://wileyonlinelibrary.com).

Call for Proposals

The ASHE Higher Education Report Series is actively looking for proposals. We encourage you to contact one of the editors, Dr. Kelly Ward (kaward@wsu.edu) or Dr. Lisa Wolf-Wendel (lwolf@ku.edu), with your ideas.

Assessing Meaning Making and Self-Authorship

Recent Titles